Maria Mendonça

A WORLD AGO

MEMORIES OF A
MADEIRA CHILDHOOD

Transcribed and Edited by
Edward Lee

W0007101

ELM VILLAGE ARTS
London

ELM VILLAGE ARTS
London

First published 2016
This revised edition published in Great Britain 2019

Paperback ISBN: 978-1-9160457-3-6

A CIP record for this book is available from the British Library.

Formatting and cover design by
Bhavnish Kanojia: *Digital Design*

ELM VILLAGE ARTS
www.elmvillagearts.co.uk

A World Ago

Passamos a grande ilha da Madeira,
Que do muito arvoredo assim se chama,
Das que nós povoamos, a primeira,
Mais célebre por nome que por fama:
Mas nem por ser do mundo a derradeira
Se lhe aventajam quantas Vênus ama,
Antes, sendo esta sua, se esquecera
De Cipro, Gnido, Pafos e Citera.

"Os Lusiadas", Canto V – Estância 5 Luis de Camões

We passed the great island of Madeira,
which is so called because of its great woodlands,
and is the first of those our people settled on.
It is more famous for its name than for Classical legend.
But it would not have been the last in the world of the many islands
Venus loves,
if they had found it first.
Had it been hers, she would have forgotten
Cyprus, Cnidos, Paphos and Cithera.

Contents

Introduction

In August 1990 my wife and I had just moved house. We were both working, so, for the first time in our lives, we engaged a cleaner. A friend employed a lady from Madeira, who was unable to take on the work, but recommended a colleague, also from Madeira. Her name was Maria Camara,(her husband's surname) and she came from a small village, Silveira, near Santana, in the far north of the island.

I arrived back from work one day to find her being shown around the house by my wife. She was a very Mediterranean-looking woman, with minimal English. So my wife, a language teacher, was deploying all her teaching skills to use our holiday Portuguese, in order to communicate. The lady seemed not only very unimpressed by us or the house, but strongly to disapprove. We wondered what we had let ourselves in for.

She began work, and was vigorous and highly competent — an old Irish friend, doing some DIY for us exclaimed "Jeez, can she clean!" Then one day, as I came home, my wife rushed up and whispered "She's singing!" We knew it would work out.

Over the years we got to know each other better, and one of the most touching moments we have ever had was when we were invited by Maria to a party. When we arrived, we realised that we were the only people there who were not family.

With the improvement in her English — not easy when you are working very long hours in order to survive — communication grew, to the benefit of both sides, and it became obvious that Maria's initial severity was in fact a sign of immense embarrassment and uncertainty.

I gave her English lessons, and prepared her for an exam, which she confessed was the first she had ever taken in her life. She was petrified, but fortunately one of the examiners, who knew me, as I worked at the same university, was very welcoming to her. So she relaxed, and to her great delight, passed well.

Then at a certain point I started working from home much more, and we got into the habit of finishing her morning with a cup of coffee and what she called a "shout." I was puzzled until I realised that she had misheard "chat"! By this time I had met all of her close family, and so she would talk about them and Madeira, and her life there.

Then one day she mentioned grinding grain by hand, using a stone that they turned. Suddenly, a memory came up of a picture in a book I had when I was about nine, The Story of Britain told in pictures. *It was a Neolithic woman using a ... quern. I don't think I had seen or used the word since.*

It suddenly came to me that this modern woman, with mobile phone and a car, had grown up in a society which had not changed, certainly in centuries, and in some respects in millennia. In one lifetime of half a century she had experienced what in Britain had been three centuries of change.

Furthermore, because the members of that community had been illiterate (her mother still is and makes a mark, not a signature), all knowledge was orally transmitted. So Maria's experiences were the result of an unbroken chain back to those Neolithic women (and as it turns out, before). If no one passed on the knowledge, it was gone forever, and its existence might not even be guessed at.

Maria's experience, if not unique, was certainly rare, as she was born in 1960. In the wider world, it was the year in which the heart pacemaker and the laser entered our lives. In the United States John F. Kennedy won the U.S. Presidential Election, being the youngest person to have done so. In the same year the United States decided to send 3,500 U.S. troops to Vietnam, the start of a war which scarred the nation.

Maria's life was so different – effectively in an earlier century -because Portugal was still one of the poorer and least technically advanced countries in Europe. It was the more so because it remained locked in the Fascist era. She was born on an island, Madeira, distant from the mainland. She lived in the area round Santana, a town very removed from the relative modernity of Funchal, the capital. And the village where she lived, Silveira, was an outpost which was even more remote, where there was not only no electricity, but no road. Life there was still in many respects medieval.

The thought of the distance she had come was awesome. I felt it should be recorded and shared with others – or at the least, passed on to her children and grandchildren, which is what Maria thought of when I put the idea to her. So this is her story.

Memories do not present themselves in the neat sequences of a Maths textbook, so we switched on my digital recorder and Maria talked. I would at times ask a question to clarify a point, or would put forward a question that I felt would interest a reader.

The recordings had first to be transcribed — the most laborious part of the project for me, because I am not an audio typist.

I then edited what we had. Next we read my version together, with Maria correcting points, and often being reminded of other relevant material. This is the version you have here.

In editing, the most important principle for me was that everything should be Maria's thoughts and words. So I have not added or taken out material.

Often whole sections could be left where they occurred in the transcription, but because of our work method, there were times when it was clear that a different order would be more helpful to a reader.

The other thing was that Maria was using her second language and was thinking and being moved by her memories, so there were grammatical errors. As her education had been very limited, her speech was also unmodified by the conventions of written language. And there were some vocabulary issues — how many readers would care to give the word for sickle in any language than their own? So I have tidied up such matters, to avoid unnecessary distractions.

To those who would criticise the informal or unliterary style of her story I make no apologies. The aim is not to create an academic or literary text but to give as far as possible the sense of sitting with a real person, Maria, and hearing her talk about her past. There is a real challenge for an editor in doing this without either altering the original too much, or becoming boringly repetitive.

I have provided each chapter with a short introduction — clearly distinguished by the use of italics. This is to prepare the reader for matters which Maria takes for granted — I suspect not many readers would happily talk about the Salazar regime or the milling of cereals.

The rest is pure Maria.

Edward Lee, Editor.

My Grandparents

The first arrivals in Madeira, after 1420, were a mixture of minor nobility, some fairly poor families and some former prisoners. Maria has no knowledge of the history of her family before her grandparents, so we cannot know from which (if any) of these groups they were descended, but it is clear that the families have been there for generations.

Few readers are likely to be familiar with the production of linen, which has long been known to provide clothing which is hardwearing but cool and comfortable, and bed linen which lasts, but becomes steadily softer with use.

Maria's grandmother was responsible for the whole process. She first grew flax plants, which she then turned into thread, before weaving it into cloth. For this she used a hand loom, a device which in England had rapidly been made obsolete by the invention of the power loom by Edmund Cartwright in 1784-5.

Maria's account is fascinating because she describes processes which had been the same for thousands of years. The Ancient Egyptians used linen widely, and there is evidence that hand loom weaving of the sort she describes was practiced in the Neolithic era (about 7000 BC). Maria's ancestors could neither read nor write, so what she describes are the last moments of thousands of years of oral tradition.

My mum was ten when her mother passed away, and her father died when she was twenty, so I never knew them.

My mum was the oldest of five children. Everyone said my grandfather was a good man, but after my grandmother died, he married again and my mum's stepmother was not nice to them.

But I remember my father's parents very well. We saw them often, and I helped my grandfather on his farm, when my father was away in Jersey working. He was a friendly sort of person. He wore a waistcoat, trousers and a hat made with wool, with flaps to cover the ears when it was cold – he had them on top of the hat when it was warm. My father was not his oldest child, but he was the oldest boy and they got on very well.

My grandmother was very different from her husband – certainly more noisy! But she was very kind. When I was a teenager, and even when I was married, she always wanted to give me things – some money or a gift, such as linen tea towels she had made.

She was kind to other people, too. I remember there was a wall outside her house, which was the right height for people to put down their burden, when they were carrying something on their head or their shoulders.

It may seem strange to someone today, but that was normal in those days; in fact when I go there I still do it. You would carry anything from the farm – grass or hay for the cows, potatoes, wood. Water I carried in a big pot on one shoulder. You carried big bundles, such as hay, across both shoulders. But you would carry a basket on top of your head. At least, you would if you were a woman – the men always used their shoulders. If you had something on, such as a cardigan, you would put that under the basket, or you could use a sack. Then if it was raining you could put it over you and on your shoulders to keep you dry. If you didn't have a sack, you could use leaves, such as cabbage or grass, to put on your head. But sometimes you didn't have anything to put under the load. It may seem that it is a very tough and rough way to carry things, but then it was normal.

My grandparents had some land at a distance from their house, near the woods. They didn't normally go there, because it was a long way, and in summer they let it grow, so there was grass for the cows. When you cut grass for the cows, you rolled it up. It was soft, so you put in on your head.

Life for both sets of grandparents was very different from how things are nowadays. They all made their living from the land. Nowadays young people in Madeira don't want that sort of life – they prefer a nine to five job in the town.

It was a very traditional way of life and also they were self-sufficient. They had to be, because to get to the city you had to walk a long way, and of course you had to pay for what you wanted. My grandparents were used to walking much further than people do nowadays, along very narrow, rough or steep paths. Also, people were poor, so you only bought things when you really had to. For instance, my father said that they used to go to the sea to get salt.

My grandparents had a wood fire for their whole life – they never had gas or electricity. And they didn't have running water. We had to go to a spring to fetch water for them – I remember my father used to say "Go and get some water for my parents!" My grandparents had a lot of grandchildren and anyone who went to their house had to go to the spring to fetch water.

They had a tank made of cement and you put the water into that, and they took from it when they wanted – but nothing was wasted. You would wash the potatoes and then use the water for something else. At our house it was the same. When you came in, you would wash your feet – my grandparents had a wooden bowl for that – some wood is waterproof – but all the children had to wash in the same water!

At that time there were no showers. You used to wash yourself in the bowl to go to church on Sunday – we boiled the water on the wood fire and washed ourselves that way. But during the week you just washed your feet and went to bed.

As I said, at first my grandparents had a wooden bowl. Then they had aluminium and then plastic bowls. The aluminium was better, because it lasts for longer – plastic breaks easily.

Being farmers, they had all sorts of animals. They had a few sheep – there were a few others like that in the village. But most of the sheep were up on the mountains – there were shepherds there who owned them and looked after them. In June they would shear them for wool. They brought them into a big pen in the village to do the shearing. That day was a festival, which we called *Tosquia* (Shearing), and people sang and drank wine.

Some people also killed a sheep at Easter for meat. But lamb was not so common as a dish with us then. The main meat was pork. So my grandparents had pigs. They had one huge pig for breeding – every year they kept one to breed. They used to kill the pigs at Christmas time, and the meat they didn't eat at Christmas, they used to salt to eat later. It was only later that people started to kill the pigs at other times of the year.

My grandparents also had cows. They milked them every night and morning. The night milking you keep to the next day and mix it with the morning milk. You churn it – you shake it about in a special sort of barrel with a handle (the churn) and it makes cream on one side, and the rest – the buttermilk – comes to the other side.

Because they had a lot of cows and they wanted to sell the cream, they took it to a local dairy, where they had a big churn to separate the cream and buttermilk. The dairy measured the number of litres people brought each day and kept a record, and then paid them for it at end of the month. They sent the cream away to be made into butter – we only had butter for ourselves at Christmas. The buttermilk you brought home and fed to the pigs.

As I said, the milk you left with the dairy was taken to be sold. At that time there were no made-up roads, so there were people who carried it in 20 litre pots on their shoulders to the nearest main road. Later there was a lorry that came every morning to take the untreated whole milk.

Then things changed. Some people stuck with the old ways for a while, but now there are only two people in the whole area who keep cows.

There were other animals. My grandparents had goats – and my father kept a goat too. There were dogs and cats but not as pets, like people do now. They were farm animals, to catch rats and so on. And we had a lot of rabbits, for their meat. They were kept in a hutch made of any spare bits of wood. Unlike in other Mediterranean areas, there were no donkeys, nor geese, and ducks were not common.

But there were certainly hens and chickens! Some they kept for eggs, and some they kept separate to raise for meat. But it was not like nowadays with Kentucky Fried and so on – they were killed at the end of the year and for special occasions. They were certainly "free range", because they didn't have a special coop or barn. They went everywhere. They came into the garden and even into the house – right into the kitchen. I hated it, because they made a mess and a smell everywhere. There were a lot of strong smells then, because even the pigs grew up next to the house. Nowadays people don't let that happen, because of the smell.

We didn't have any vehicles such as wheelbarrows or carts –nothing with wheels. Instead we used a lot of wicker baskets in lots of different sizes, with a handle. There were a lot of *vimeiro* (willow) trees around, so we made the baskets ourselves – it was cheaper. We also sold some of the wicker to people who made baskets for a living. Plastic containers came later.

The reason there were no barrows or trolleys was because the paths were very narrow and uneven. Later when they built the roads in Santana, people started to use carts with wooden wheels which they made themselves.

In my grandparents' time some transportation was done by using oxen – that was when they had something big to move. There were three people who owned oxen in our area. They worked every day, and there was plenty of work for them, transporting things for us. But of course we had to pay them. They didn't have ox carts, but a sort of sledge – we called it a *corsa de boi*. There were two pieces of wood that they made smooth, for runners, and the oxen pulled it. They used them on the land, and also on the main street which was not smooth and made up with tarmac, like it is now. It was cobbled and the runners slid over the stones.

It is interesting to see that nowadays they have something similar for tourists in Funchal. They have sledges, but they are pushed from behind by men over cobbled streets which are very steep.

One big thing they used the *corsa de boi* for was to carry logs for us. There were a lot of trees on the farms. So you had wood to cook, to make a fire for warmth in winter, and to build houses. But there was a timber factory near us. So my grandparents and parents used to cut the trees into logs to send to the factory, where they cut them up into timber for building and making furniture and so on. Now we are not allowed to cut trees without permission from the Government.

It mattered where your farm was situated. I have an auntie, she is called Tia Maria (Auntie Maria) and she is my father's sister. She lives close to the sea. So her farm was lower down than ours, which was in the mountains. That meant it was warmer there, and crops ripened before ours, and she would bring us bananas and grapes to give to my grandmother. My auntie was very kind, but her husband was very mean, even though he had plenty of money. But she always found a way to get something behind his back to give us.

As I said, my grandparents were self-sufficient: they even made their own *aguardente* – that's a strong alcoholic spirit! But I particularly remember that they made their own clothes, bedclothes, mats for the floors and so on. Most of this was made of linen.

They grew their own flax. When you gather the flax plant is very dark, so first they laid it out in the sun to bleach it. After a while my grandmother would take the fibres and work them by hand to get threads that were the thickness she needed. Some could be thick, say for mats. Then there was the cloth from which they made shirts for the men, and sheets and dresses. But some was very fine, like silk, and that took a lot of work and care. After that she rolled the thread into a ball.

Next you had a *tear* (loom). It was a wooden machine, with threads across. There were two lines of threads in parallel. In your hand you held the *lançadeira* (shuttle) which holds a thread. The loom also had two foot pedals. So you used both your feet and your hands. First you passed the shuttle up between the horizontal threads. Then you used one pedal which moved a piece of wood, to bring the threads together to make them very tight. You use the other pedal to switch the position of the horizontal lines. Then you pass the shuttle back down.

My grandmother made the threads into strips of material that were all the same size, about half the size of a table. If you wanted something wide, such as a sheet, you sewed two strips together. When she made an article, Grandmother always sewed by hand, stitching with a needle. She wanted me to learn, but I wasn't interested. But later I did learn to do crocheting, sewing, stitching and knitting. We also had mats and bed covers which were a sort of quilt – not made from a single piece of linen, but from small flat pieces, less wide than a finger. You sewed them together by hand. They were very warm.

The tradition then was that every girl had to have some linen – clothes, sheets, blankets, bedspreads and towels – to be ready for when she married. My grandmother had a big wooden box to keep it all in and in good condition. Even now I have some things from my own *enxoval* (trousseau).

One is a linen christening shawl which was made by my mother. It is made of white linen and is decorated with embroidered leaves. It is a beautiful object, and in many families the shawl becomes an heirloom. It was a tradition to give girls one for their wedding trousseau.

At the christening you wrap the baby in the shawl, and you light a special candle, to burn during the ceremony. When you put it out, you save it until the child's first Holy Communion, when you light it again. People like to save their candle, and so my son saved his until the christening of his first child.

My Parents

Maria's parents continued the traditional way of life. Being born in the 1930s, they spent their lives until about the age of forty in a remote village under the fascist regime of Antonio Salazar. But this seems to have had little obvious impact on their daily life.

The exception was military conscription, which could be two years and was extended because of increasing demands of colonial wars. The importance of the US involvement in Vietnam during the period is widely known. Less well known is the fact that by 1974 a million and a half Portuguese men had undertaken service overseas. One of these was Maria's father, who spent his Army years in Goa. The dislike and fear of conscription led to a lot of migration, especially to France.

In this chapter we also hear about land disputes, including the use and moving of boundary stones. This problem goes back to Biblical times: "Cursed is the one who moves his neighbour's boundary stone." (Deuteronomy 27:17)

It may surprise many readers to hear that Maria's parents were cousins. Cousin marriage is legal in the UK, but is discouraged medically because of health risk for the children. In Maria's youth, the Catholic church prohibited cousin marriage, but could and did make dispensations for such unions. Happily all the children and grandchildren of Maria's parents were born without medical issues.

My father, Manuel Marques Mendonça, was born in 1934. His father's name was João, though it was very common for the father and son to have the same name. So when an official letter arrives for the son you often see *filho* (son) in the address. But it was also a tradition in those days for the first boy child to be called Manuel and the first girl Maria, as I am. Afterwards they got TV, other names became more popular.

My father didn't go to school (at that time it was not compulsory) and so did not learn to read or write, but after he was married, he learned to write his name. But for maths, though he never wrote numbers, he had a brilliant brain. He could do it all in his head.

After he reached 18, he was conscripted into the Army – you had to go. They had first to go to the barracks for one day to be observed and tested. Nobody wanted to be exempted, because they felt that if you were not accepted, you were not a proper man. They were called up later, when they were 20.

Of course, many men didn't want to go. They had travel a long way, to the colonies – my father was sent to Goa in India – and then there were wars and a lot of men were away for a long time – you weren't always sure how long it would be. A lot of parents thought it was goodbye forever, and it was always very painful for the family. So some parents sent their children abroad, for instance to Brazil.

So my father went to the Army when he was 20. Then, after he left the Army, he spent about five years in Madeira. After that, he went to Mozambique, when I was about six months old. I still remember the small case he brought back with him from Mozambique – it was in our house for many years. It was good quality, but very small. Recently I asked my mum about it and she said he got it when he went to do his military service.

When my father had a conversation with people, he could sit down and talk and talk, but he was not a person who showed his important emotions much. He always cared for us even till late in life, but he was not a person who showed his love for us. He could be quite strict. He didn't like his children to mess around. He always wanted us to work and to come home and not go to parties and festivals or mix in that sort of life.

He was careful with money, but my mother bought the things we children needed – she knew when and where to buy. I never heard him complain about what my mum spent. He tried to give the children what they needed.

So when I was young, we were not rich, but our clothes and footwear were a little better than a lot of other people around. For instance, some people didn't even have a pair of boots – I remember myself walking around without boots. In fact, a lot of the time we didn't feel that we needed shoes. But sometimes, when you were working, you needed boots. Well, at a certain point my father bought us plastic boots, one pair for my mum and one pair for me. We still had to be careful with them. I was a big girl and so mine were the same size as my mum's, so often I wore my mum's boots! And when they wore down, my father mended them for us – some people had to go to the *sapateiro* (shoemaker), but he mended them himself.

He was careful with money, but for the sake of his children, not just for his own pocket. I remember we had a neighbour who looked quite rich, but the children were much poorer than us, and when they grew up a bit, they had to buy their own clothes. I didn't have to buy my own clothes when I was a teenager, not until I was married.

One thing I remember well is that when my father came home from working, he liked his food to be ready! In the morning, it was no problem. When you go to feed the animals and milk the cows, you know more or less what time you will come back.

But lunchtime was a bit different. My father didn't have a watch. But he knew the time from the sun. He used to put a stick in the ground and he knew from the shadow when it was midday. When the shadow was on one side, it was before midday, and when it was on the other side, it was after midday. But when there was no shadow, it was exactly midday.

In the evening, when he came back, there was another meal. He would come home when it got dark. We had to come back then, too – he didn't want us to be back late. Sometimes he went to work for the day for other people. On those days we ate in the evening what was left over from the lunchtime. We liked it then, because we had coffee with corn meal or cold or fried potatoes. We didn't have coffee every day and at that time for us, we felt it was a good meal. But he wasn't happy about that – he used to say "That is not a proper meal!"

In some ways my father was a very individual person. For instance, he liked tea, which was unusual. I think it may be because he had been in India. It was leaves, not teabags! He also felt that tea was good for the cows, when they were ill. He would boil the tea and then he added some special herbs, and lemon and orange leaves.

Another original thing he did was that he grew things which other people didn't. One was tomatoes – maybe he got the idea in Mozambique. Nobody in Santana grew tomatoes then – maybe they did in the south of Madeira, but not where we were, in the north. He went to the city and brought the seeds home and planted them.

My mother, Maria de Jesus Marques da Silva, was born in 1937. Her mother was Lucia de Jesus. My grandfather was Manuel Marques da Silva. Back home we use the middle name – here he would just be Manuel Mendonça.

I remember naming sometimes caused problems. There was a couple who worked in the Registry Office for many years, who did whatever they felt like! So if you went to register a child, they might just decide "No, not this name!" This happened to my cousin. She didn't know until she got to school that she was registered under a different name!

My mother's mother died when my mother was ten, and her father passed away when she was twenty, so she had to look after her brothers and sisters. She had a hard life until she married my father.

But things have not always been easy between my mum and her family. One of her sisters has always been difficult. There were several court cases about who owned property and land.

There were two houses and my aunt had one and my mother the other.

The problem was that at that time they didn't keep a land register, but even afterwards, when this changed, people didn't always follow it. In the old days you needed to put a stone at each of the four corners of the land round your house with your name on it. And yet greedy people would move the stones. But people remembered, and at last the person who moved stones died. And when people went to the funeral, they said that they saw the earth on the grave was lower than the others around. They said the earth was not enough to cover the dead person, that the earth on the grave was very shallow, because they always stole it during their lives!

Another problem came when my aunt sold the house that was next door to my mum's house. Normally you offer the neighbour the first chance to buy. But my aunt didn't do this and sold the property to someone who was a very bad neighbour. He made claims, and without a proper record at the Land Registry, it depends on memories of the past. Even so he lost a court case. But he didn't give up, and one time he bribed a young man to be a witness. The dispute had happened 60 years before, so he was far too young! Finally the matter went to a High Court in Lisbon, and the man lost that case too.

My mother is very good at embroidery. I don't know if she did it before she got married. What I do know is that when she was in Mozambique, she had a lot of time and she did a lot of embroidery. She made towels, and dresses for me. We still have many of the things.

When we came back to Madeira, she got to know a lady in the area who went to the city every month and brought material and articles from a factory for people to embroider. My mum used to do it in the middle of the day, between meals, and especially after lunch, particularly if it was hot weather.

She got a pension from it, which has been very useful. If you didn't have a job, you had to pay for your pension, and of course she was a housewife. But she got paid for the embroidery she had done, and when you earned above a certain amount, they made a compulsory deduction and you started to get points towards your pension. So in the end she got a good one.

My mother married my father after he came out of the Army. I believe my parents were interested in each other before he went into the Army. Sometimes the young man wanted to get married before he went, to make sure the girl was his! My mum had her family to look after, so that wasn't possible. But she said that once my father came back, he didn't waste any time!

At that time if a boy wanted to see a girl, he had to ask permission from the girl's parents. My mother and father were cousins, so they knew each other from childhood. That meant they were already friends and he could see her more easily. Even so, in the past he hadn't come often to my mum's house, because his parents were a bit higher class than my mum's. But once he was back, he found a way!

I don't think he brought her presents – it wasn't normal in those days, because people were very poor – but he brought things from the land for the family.

Then one time he came to my grandparents' house and he talked privately to her father. She knew something was going on, though her father didn't say anything to her. But the next day my father came again. And this time he brought five litres of wine in a *garafão* (flask) to give to my mum's parents, so as to get the opportunity to keep coming to their house. Then it came to Christmas time. They killed a pig and Mum's father invited him to come to the feast. And from then on they kept on meeting.

There were other boys who liked my mum, but she wasn't interested in them. There was one fellow in particular. Because she didn't fancy him, she told him that she was too young to get married. But there was none of that with my father. As soon as he came home, she accepted him. When this other fellow heard, he complained to her: "You said you were too young. So I've been waiting for you. And now you go with this guy. Leave him and come to me." She refused so he threatened "If you don't marry me, you will never see me again." She still refused him, so he went away, I think to Brazil.

Then Mum's father passed away, and so she waited a while, during the period of mourning. But when she was 21, they got married. It did not matter that they were cousins, but in those cases when cousins got married, they had to contribute some money to the church.

But people said that when you married a cousin, this could have an effect for five generations – not just the first generation. One of my cousins was our neighbour and she had two blind children, which people thought was because of a past marriage between cousins. I have a sister in Jersey – she married her cousin. Her son is OK, but you never know.

It was not a big wedding! At that time they had a tradition that if you didn't have a big party, you didn't marry in your local church. You went to the city. Well, because her father had died recently and she had no parents, they didn't want to make a big occasion of it. So they went to the city to get married.

They had to walk, because there was no transport. When they got there, there weren't many people there, because it was too far – I think there was just someone to sign the book as a witness. My dad's father went with him, though.

They went to a church – at that time you didn't go to a Registry Office – and in fact, I was married in the same church as my mum. But that church had a bad reputation; people said that when people went there to marry, they were not virgins!

Sadly, people don't care about these things now. They don't respect religion and they just want a party. You can even marry when you already have children. But at that time it was different. Of course people misbehaved – they always did – but they covered these things up.

Well, after the ceremony, they walked back to Santana, and when they got home, they went straight away to do the farm work and to cut wood to cook – no party, nothing!

Mozambique

The Portuguese had set up trading settlements in what is now Mozambique as early as 1498. Over the centuries they extended their control, but only finally occupied most of the territory in 1918.

The economy of Mozambique expanded rapidly during the 1950s and 1960s. This drew thousands of Portuguese settlers to the country. Subsidies were then offered by the Estado Novo *regime of Dr Salazar to encourage people to settle in Angola or Mozambique. It was presumably this offer which attracted Maria's father. Interestingly, there was a special payment for Portuguese men who agreed to marry an African woman; clearly this would not have been well received by Maria's mother!*

Maria lived in Mozambique for eight years, so some readers may be surprised that Maria does not mention either military forces or war. This is because she lived in Baixo Limpopo, in the far south of the country, whereas the FRELIMO *campaign (the African liberation movement of the region) was based far to the north.*

Maria does not know why her father decided to leave Mozambique. But we do know that the had a radio, and so may well have heard news of what was happening elsewhere and at home. In September 1968, a month before Maria's eighth birthday, Antonio Salazar was replaced by Marcelo Caetano, it was claimed for health reasons. There had been growing opposition to the regime for ten years before this, and on 25 November 1968 thousands of students from Porto and Lisbon, inspired by student unrest all over Europe, gathered in Coimbra for protest meetings. It therefore seems plausible that Maria's father realised that the situation in Mozambique was going to worsen, while back home things might get better, and so decided to leave.

Whilst one should not attempt to glamourise the relations between the colonial power and the indigenous population, it is accurate to claim that Portuguese policy towards the African population was different in important respects from that of other colonial powers, and from that in neighbouring South Africa. (see Background 1 – Some Portuguese History, *page 141 for details).*

I was born in Madeira, but we moved to Mozambique when I was a baby of nine months old. Of course, I don't remember what happened and why we went, but I think my father heard an announcement that the government wanted people to go. I know that my father always thought about the future. Also, he had been in the Army, so maybe he had good memories and wanted to travel again – when you have been somewhere else, your mind is more extended.

I don't have many memories of Africa – we came back to Madeira when I was eight. My mum said we were in Baixo Limpopo and we lived far from the city, Lourenço Marques. But I remember the street where we lived. There were houses opposite each other, just one row on each side of the road. Our house was at the end of the street, and when you walked on from there you came to the farmland. And I remember what the houses looked like – it was a huge house, ours. The houses were built of bricks, not wood. I think they were well furnished and we didn't have to buy anything. We had electricity in Mozambique and we had indoor toilets, because it was a big modern house.

Between the houses there was a big *forno* – a bread oven – everyone could go there and make their bread – everyone knew how to make bread at that time.

When my father got to Mozambique, I don't think he owned the land where he was working – everyone had one plot to work. It was flat land, like a desert. But they were growing rice. There was a lot of water – I don't know where from – because you grow rice in water. In the rice fields it was very hot. And because the water was quite deep, my father rolled up his trousers and wore nothing on his feet – certainly no boots.

I have one memory of a big group of people in a row in the water. They were thinning out the rice plants – you take the plants out and re-plant them in empty spaces. And they used to put a string with empty cans on it around the edge of the field, to make a noise to frighten the birds, so they wouldn't eat the rice.

I remember very well my father being outside and me being with him. My mum says that my father always took us with him. He didn't show much that he loved us, but inside the love was there, and he kept us with him wherever he went. And though at that time you didn't have a lot of food, like there is now, he always saved something for us children from anything he got.

But one problem for my parents was that they only grew rice. So my mum says that for six months of the year they didn't work, and my father was idle. But my mum always found something to do! She did a lot of embroidery, and she spent a lot of time talking to people.

There was no hospital and just one corner shop. I don't remember a church. They just built the new houses for us settlers. And there was no school, so I was with my parents all the time. If my mum went to a friend's house, I had to go with her.

We had some neighbours who had travelled on the same boat as us from Madeira too – there were a lot of Madeira people there. For example, opposite our house there was a couple from Madeira. The lady had a boy almost the same age as me and another boy – just the two children – we played together. She was a good lady and very good with her hands. She did lots of things for us and made clothes for my mum and me and my brother and sister, even after we went back to Madeira.

My mum had another friend with four children. The adults always talked and I wanted to be with them. I don't know if I was a good child. I think I was good with some and not with others!

There was another lady I remember well. Once my sister was very ill and became very thin and she always asked for Mum and this lady. She and her husband didn't have children and were very good to us. But it was very sad, because she once asked my mum to give her one of us – naturally, my mother refused.

I can remember the Africans – they were black people. The Africans spoke their own language, but I don't remember any of it. At the end of the road where we lived there were bushes and trees and the black people lived there. I remember that their houses were built with mud.

I recall being with them, perhaps not many times, but I have a strong memory of it. My mum said the black people were very surprised to see the white people there, but they became friends with us, and we with them. They worked for us and they came to our house. They loved me – I was a bit chubby and they took me to be around with them. I recall that they cooked in different ways because they didn't have our facilities.

The Africans didn't work in the house, because my mum had time to do the housework, but they worked in the fields. I think for them it looked like they started life with us; I mean they had a family, but no life. They just lived in the forest, and wore just one piece of clothing. They didn't know how to work the land; we taught them to farm and they worked for us. I am sure my parents paid them, but I don't know how much. The government paid my parents. I see now that we could do nothing for ourselves – we were told what to do and that was that.

When the black people cooked corn flour, they just boiled water and added it and they felt it was cooked, but we felt that it had to cook for a while. And I remember that then they took the cornmeal and squeezed it in their hands and ate it.

Another thing I remember was that they had a big pot and they crushed things in it with a big pole, and while they worked it, they carried the children on their back. It was always women who did that work. And as they worked, they made a noise – "Ooof!" When I came back to Madeira people used to ask me to do that – to make the noise – and they laughed. And I had an African accent, and that made them laugh too.

Though we were in Africa, I don't remember any African animals, except a couple of monkeys. As I said, it was a rather desert place – no lions or elephants or things like that. But there was a house opposite, which was empty, and there were insects inside that made a lot of noise. They had long wings and we were curious and wanted to see such things.

I don't remember any special food. But I know I drank condensed milk – we didn't have fresh milk – and of course it lasts longer. My mother may have mixed it with water. I can see the tin now in my mind. So when I went back to Madeira, I didn't like real milk!

I know now that there was a war at that time in Mozambique between FRELIMO and our Army, but I don't recall any soldiers or war or trouble where I was.

One time I broke my leg, and the nearest hospital was in Lourenço Marques, the big city, and there was no public transport. But the man at the corner shop where people bought supplies had a van and he took us to the hospital. My mum couldn't come to visit me very often, because she had the other children to look after, but my father always tried to visit, though he had to travel miles.

While we were in Mozambique, my mum told us about my family and their names. I was interested because the people around us didn't have those names – names like Filomena, Ascensão, Catarina, Piedade – they were strange to us.

Life was better there, but my mum never liked it. She had looked after children from a young age, and she was used to being busy – she was always busy – but in Mozambique there wasn't so much to do.

When I was nearly eight, we left Mozambique and came back to Madeira. My mum said she wanted to come back, but because the government had organised this trip, they didn't want us to leave and wouldn't let us go back home. None of the people who went out there together came back early – my father was the only one. But in Madeira he had a place to live and he had land. Lots of the others didn't.

So my father said he wanted to go on holiday, but his real intention was to leave the country and never go back. I remember my father had luggage and a big wooden box with all of our things inside that he could pack. My mum said they left the curtains on the windows, so the people wouldn't get suspicious when they left. But when he got to the port, someone had reported him and they let my mum go onto the boat, but they detained my father. He was so furious, that someone he knew had done that.

My mum cried all the time on the boat with us and spent most of the days in her cabin; she didn't go around the boat. There were entertainments, but my mum didn't enjoy any of it – she was so sad to leave her husband behind. But I was nearly eight years old and there was my brother and my other two sisters, so we loved to explore the ship. I remember we went out of the cabin to go to eat. There were big wide stairs, and one time I felt sick on the stairs, and I vomited, because I was seasick!

After we got back to Madeira, my father followed, maybe a month later. I don't know how he got out. But people from the government came to our house – they wanted to send us back to Mozambique. Whenever anyone like that came, my father had to hide.

My father knew who informed on him. I don't know why the man did it – I think the reason was just that he was a bad person, or jealous of my father in some way. My mum said that years later my father met him in Madeira. He was still angry with the man. My father confronted him but he ran away!

After the revolution all the people still in Mozambique had a hard time, because by then they were more settled and they were growing more crops. So they became refugees and many went to South Africa. Many others came back home. My mum was glad they came back before that, though she often had to say to people that we had been in Mozambique, but we weren't refugees – we had come home before things changed.

At School

The picture Maria gives of her education in the 60s and 70s is very different from what was happening elsewhere in the world. In 1965 the Labour government took the policy decision to make British secondary schools comprehensive, as distinct from the previous division between grammar schools, where admission was by competitive examination, and secondary modern schools for all other pupils

Meanwhile, Maria went to school during the Salazar regime (the Estado Novo*). Dr Salazar believed that education was not suitable for most people – he claimed that it destroyed their traditional and religious values. He felt that higher education should be reserved for a minority (of which he, originally a professor at the University of Coimbra, naturally was one). These attitudes were reflected in slogans of the time such as "Blessed are those who forget their first letters and return to the shovel!" and "To teach how to read is to corrupt the essence of our race!"*

During Maria's school years the foundations of a new approach to education, based on digital technology, were being created in the United States by Seymour Papert. He started from the education theories of Jean Piaget, and sought to develop the autonomy of the child through the use of Logo, *a a specially created programming language, which was used to control a small mobile robot, the "Logo Turtle."*

By contrast, Maria's account is highly reminiscent of the descriptions of schooling to be found in the works of Charles Dickens and D H Lawrence.

During her account she also mentions an old children's game (known in Britain as Knucklebones or Jacks) which has a continuous tradition dating back to the Ancient Greeks.

In Mozambique there was no schooling, so we didn't have the opportunity to learn anything. But in Portugal you started school when you were seven. So when I came back to Madeira, at the age of eight, I knew nothing and I was a year behind.

When I went to school I couldn't even hold a pencil. At eight years of age, the teacher had to show me how. To teach us how to write, the teacher would write a letter of the alphabet and we had to write on top it. Then the teacher would write a line of some words or some vowels and we had to write on top of that and then copy underneath on paper. But we also had a slate, so you could rub it out easily.

We did have books, though. The teacher brought the books from the town, but we had to buy them. Even so, I remember in Year 3 that most of the children got a book but I didn't. And it took a long time to get another, because it was not like now, when there are piles of books. So the months passed and I was behind – that's probably why I had to do that year again. Then suddenly – I don't know how – I got a second hand copy, I think because my Mum talked to someone, who had already passed the class. That was lucky, because mostly the books weren't in good condition at the end of the year, so you couldn't pass them on.

I don't remember my first day at school, but I do know that I was very shy, as a child, for the whole time I was in school, and even afterwards. People used to tease me because I was big. And I was new in the country, new in the class, and I had no friends – everything was new. This happened straightaway, as soon as I returned to Madeira. Now I can I see that it had a huge impact on my everyday life, and that I didn't have the confidence to express or say what I thought.

We lived outside the village. Cars couldn't get there, so to get to the nearest town we had to walk for maybe half an hour or so. But the school was quite near – maybe 300 yards. We went to school from Monday to Friday. We started at 9 am and I seem to remember we finished at 1pm and another class started at 2 – so we didn't have lunch at school. But I remember that at break time – I forget how long the break was – maybe half an hour – I often came home for a little while to eat something.

To go to school we wore our dresses and on top a sort of white housecoat, like a doctor's, called a *bata*. Everyone had to wear it. We had to wear our best clothes for school, then, when you got home, you had to wear your old worn-out ones. Our mother never had to nag us – you knew you had to change and go to school. You had been told and that was it – you knew what you had to do. So when I came home, it was straight into the house, and change, before you talked to anyone. You didn't go the kitchen and eat – the first thing was that you had to change. Best clothes were too expensive to wear carelessly.

All the children from the village were taught in the same room; there was one room for all the classes. In the classroom I only remember a few maps on the wall. There was a cross, but no pictures, nothing else. I don't know how many children there were – but it was packed! And there was just one teacher. The small children were at the front – so they picked up things better, because they got more attention. We weren't supposed to talk, but we were in the back, and so could be inattentive! And the desks were higher, so you could hide things from the teacher, because she couldn't pay attention to us all. And you weren't allowed to go to the toilet whenever you wished – you just had to hold it!

At the start of the day there was a short prayer. This was led by the teacher – the priest didn't come into the school, but he did come to our houses. There were two candles next to the cross – which was in the middle of the hall. Some of the children would light the candles and afterwards they used a candle snuffer to put the candle out – they needed that because they couldn't reach the candles! We had to stand up and say a prayer – but I don't remember what it was.

We had to learn reading, writing, and maths. I've heard that the policy of the government at that time was: "*ler, contar, escrever*" (read, count, write). But though I've heard about and seen pictures of "*A Lição de Salazar*" (a course of texts for schools endorsed by the regime) and the *Mocidade Portuguesa* (the Salazar-ist youth movement), I don't recall anything like that.

We didn't have any lessons in singing, drawing, dancing or that sort of thing, not even in sewing or cooking. I don't remember learning about England or France or other countries, but we did learn about the Portuguese colonies, such as Angola and Guinea, and things about Portugal, as well as the discovery of Madeira, but it was hard to understand. Now it's different because you can watch TV, and people talk about things and their experiences.

We didn't have different lessons and set times, like you do in modern schools, because we had to work independently in our separate year groups.

But sometimes, for instance for Maths, you had to go and write on the blackboard. I was bad at Maths, so I often got things wrong. The teacher had a cane, and my hand was always bruised, because any time I got something wrong she hit me with it (not just me – it was the same for everybody) – bam! – on the back of my hand as I was writing.

There was a lot of caning. I remember once with the History book – the teacher corrected me, but I felt I was right, so I repeated my answer, and the teacher hit me – boom! And when we had Dictation, if you had more than so many mistakes you had to hold out your hand and the teacher hit you – not just hit you, hit you hard. We used to turn our heads away. But some children didn't. They looked at the teacher and when she made to hit them, they pulled their hand back. Sometimes they escaped the punishment, but mostly they still had to have it.

We had assemblies, not often, but I remember one, when I was in Year 4. My classmates did a presentation. One classmate's mother had died, while she was still only young, and she couldn't finish the assembly because of the emotion. She seemed to be saying "Why?" How she must have been suffering inside!

During the break the children would play. If you were like me, you didn't really get to play, because some children were the leaders, and they chose who would play with them.

Sometimes we played a game on the ground with some little stones. They were not stones out of the ground. Instead you got an old roof tile, broke it into little pieces and then rubbed them until they were smooth.

You have to put the stones on the back of your hand and then turn your hand over and catch them. If you lost, the other person took over, and when they lost, it was your turn again. Another game was that there was one stone on the ground and you had to pick that up, as well as catch the ones in the air. And there were versions where there were two or three stones on the ground to pick up. It was a good game. I've since heard it is a very old game, that the Romans played, and also it was a children's game in England in earlier times, called Knucklebones, or Jacks.

The teachers were always women. We didn't have enough teachers in the country – no one wanted to come to work in the countryside. It was hard for them – they always wanted to be in the town. So we missed a lot of time at school, because the teachers would start and then disappear. The teachers might change two or three times in a year, and there were times when we had no teachers.

They were normally young. I remember especially one young teacher we had. She was quite good, but her boyfriend used to come into the school, so of course she spent a lot of time with him.

But one teacher we had was very tough. She was a bit older, and she was very, very strict, so the children didn't like her, but at the same time we learned a lot. I can see now that she was a good teacher.

Her husband had a bakery; they baked the bread for the whole Santana area – that was as big as Euston, Camden Town, Kentish Town and Highgate put together. We had just the one bakery at that time. I remember that, because there were no roads, one of the workers at the bakery had to deliver bread to our local shop on foot. They carried the bread in a wicker basket on their shoulder.

This teacher and her husband had a big house – in fact it was a huge house with a garden – and she took us to there to study. The bakery was on the ground floor and she lived on the first floor.

When I went to primary school, if you didn't pass a year, you stayed in the same class and repeated that year. Some children were not clever enough, and they never got to the end of the curriculum. But others repeated the class and got better results the next time, and so could move on. I remember I had to repeat Year 1, and then I passed Year 2 in just the one year. Year 3 I repeated, that was two years in the same class. I passed Year 4, so I was six years in school altogether.

In Year 4 we had an old teacher – she was not old really, just mature, but she seemed old to us. She was a good teacher too. She had been teaching in the town. Her family was well known there. I can't remember her husband's work, but he had a good job – on the Council or something like that. She gave us extra time. She was teaching in two different schools – in the morning she taught us and she did the afternoon in the other school. She told us to walk there and she gave us help. As I said, she was a very good teacher. and so we passed the Year 4.

At that time Year 4 was very important. If you passed it and you lived in the city, you could go on to college. But we lived in the countryside, and so we didn't have that opportunity. It was too far. My younger sisters had more opportunity to study than me, because things changed after I had left school. Really, mostly it was a very bad education – there were too many children, and they didn't have enough teachers.

A Child at Home

Much of Maria's childhood was very different from that experienced by today's children. In a poor agricultural community it was essential that every person who could, should help.

One task, suited to a young but strong girl, was helping with the animals. But, again, her experience was very different to what happens in Britain, where there are large tracts of rich pasture land, cows graze in the fields for most to the year. In Maria's region at that time the cows were kept almost entirely in stables, and so food had to be brought to them.

This was because, first, the land was needed to grow crops, notably wheat, potatoes and maize. Second, in the Portuguese inheritance system land was divided equally between the members of a family, resulting in the ownership of many scattered small plots – there were few large fields.

In Britain the first continuous hay baler appeared in 1914. But to cut grass for the animals, Maria used a foice *(sickle), familiar to many from the flag of the former Soviet Union. It is a hand-held cutting tool, used for harvesting grain and cutting forage (grass used as animal food). It is mentioned in the Bible, but we know that it is a tool which dates at least from the Iron Age*

Maria describes the facilities which her mother had for cooking meals. These may seem to readers to be startlingly primitive, though the ingenuity of Maria's father overcame many of the problems.

But we should not be too complacent. A British survey in 1950 found that only 46 per cent of households had bathrooms, 15 per cent had no water-heating appliance, 64 per cent in London and South and East England used kettles and pans to heat water for washing, and 10 per cent in South and East England did not even have piped water. Perhaps, in a time of increasing pressure on resources, Maria's family has a a lot to teach us about imaginative responses to conservation.

When I came to Madeira, it felt strange. First of all, the houses were very different. Like I said, in Mozambique we had a big modern house with a toilet. But in Madeira the houses were much smaller. In the old days they were a triangle shape, with a thatched roof – nowadays lots of tourists come to see them. And when they had the thatched houses, they made them with three rooms. In the front part of the house you had the parents' bed, and the children slept in the room at the back. The boys were on one side and the girls on the other. Then when they built houses with brick, they built small rooms, because they is what they were used to.

But that wasn't all. My mother's parents had a house, and when they had both died, their family divided it. They had four bedrooms: my mum got one, my aunts got one each and the brother got the other one, though he was in Brazil. It was all on one floor, so for privacy, they just closed the inside doors and had a different door to get in from the outside.

When my parents married, my father went to live in the room that belonged to my mum – she still has that and bit of land. And I remember that my father extended their part of the house.

In the old days the kitchen was separate from the house because of the risk of fire. That was because it was made of wood, though inside, the fireplace was made with cement. But the kitchen could be quite a distance from the house.

When my father made the extension, he added a kitchen with a tiled roof. He built it against the wall of the extension – there was no door to the rest of the house. The door was on the outside – so if it rained when you went there, you hurried! We cooked and ate in the kitchen. At first we didn't have chairs, so my father made a bench around the table against the wall. Then he made small stools for us.

He made another kitchen before I got married. It had a *forno* (oven) for baking bread. They made it from special stones they got from the ground – I don't know the name – which keep the heat very well. Then he made a block of cement, to make a *lareira* (hearth) for cooking.

There was a metal circle for a wood fire. It was circular to keep the flames in. That meant that it was hotter, cooking took less time and you used less wood. Over it there were metal strips to make a sort of hob. This was for saucepans and frying pans – everything was boiled or fried.

Around that, at the back, he added a metal tank, that you put water in, so that the fire could heat it. After that he fixed for the water to come into the house – before that you had to go outside to get water. But now when you cooked, you had cold water, and after you heated the water, it stayed hot and you could use it for a shower.

The most important room in the house was the sitting room. We didn't use this room during the year – we just used it for a party at Christmas or a wedding or christening or when somebody special came to the house. But like I said before, the rooms were small. There was a table in the room and four chairs. It was a small table like a bedside table, or a small old fashioned writing desk. Normally, they kept it against the wall. There was a small set of shelves on it, that looked like steps. That was to save space. On the top one you had a statue of Mary or maybe a cross. At Christmas you covered the steps with a cloth, and you had the baby Jesus on the top step, with oranges and *trigo* (wheat) seedlings. Nowadays, the Baby Jesus is lying in the manger, but then it was different. He was standing up and the statue was maybe 30-40 centimetres high. Later, they made a Nativity scene on the floor, and had a Christmas tree.

One thing was we didn't have toilets like in we did in Mozambique. Our toilet was outside the house because we didn't have water inside. They just had a small storehouse to go to. Afterwards my father made a bench with wood for us to sit down. We didn't use toilet paper – we used soft grass instead. Then you put grass on top of the waste. Later we used any paper that was around, such as the bags you got when you bought something. It was rough but we were used to it.

When it was a bit full, we took it away like we did with the cows. There was a field next to the house, where you put it in the ground. Or in summer when we watered the plants, my father channelled the water to wash the waste into the ground.

That was like what we did with the cows' waste, too. Sometimes you take the waste and you spread it with water. It's good for beans, because the beans grow upwards and the waste is just in the ground. And you can do it with *milho* (corn). But we didn't do it with the potatoes. Sweet potatoes we did, but only when the leaves appeared, before the sweet potatoes grew.

When I came to England, I found it strange that they had the toilet near the front door, because in Madeira it was at the back. But when I had a house built in Madeira I wanted the toilet near the door and they didn't want to do it!

When I was young, the whole family got up at about the same time. That was about 7am, or earlier, if you had to feed the cows and milk them. My mother would be up a bit earlier because she had to see to the children and have breakfast ready for when we came back from feeding the animals. Our breakfast was normally things left over from the night before.

Lunch times varied – it depended on where my father was working. On days when we went to school, we had lunch when we came home from school, and we stayed at home for a while. You might do some chores around the house, or feed the chickens. But sometimes my father would tell us to go straight to the land to help him, maybe to water the land or something, and then you came home in the evening .

When my father was working at a distance from the house, he would normally take some food with him. But I remember one time my father was working in the mountains. He was cutting wood, because the wood in the mountains is better for making fence posts – it lasts for ages.

Well, that morning my father decided he wanted something warm for lunch, so my mum cooked some potatoes and covered them up and put them in a wicker basket, and she put something warm to drink in a flask. In fact, it was hot chocolate, which was unusual at that time. I took these things to him and something for the other men who were working with him, and my brother came too. We took it to him up the hill.

But the tracks were full of rocks and steep and narrow, so the flask kept banging against the rocks on the side of the path and the flask must have got cracked. I didn't notice that the hot chocolate had spilled all over the ground. When I realised I was so scared! I knew that when I got to him, he was waiting for it and I had none. But he wasn't angry with me.

In the evenings some people had dinner late, after it got dark, but my father didn't like that. By the time it got dark, the dinner had to be ready! Some people prayed before and after meals, but my father only had us to pray after, to thank God for the meal. I remember that my father normally wore a cap, but he always took it off before he ate. Nobody does that now.

We all went to bed at the same time. My father didn't like us to go to bed after him – he wanted us in bed early. We would eat our dinner, wash out feet, and then go to bed – you didn't do anything else.

Or rather, there was one thing. My father was not very religious – he was not very fond of priests! – but he wanted us to pray – not much, but he made us pray a little. He was in bed in the next room and he wanted to hear our voices praying. Yet we didn't hear *him* pray – he didn't pray aloud. But I'm sure he did pray, in a whisper, making his own prayers.

During the week there was always housework, and you had to feed the animals and do other farm work. This began to happen even before children went to school – as soon as you could, you did something. When children were very small and couldn't do anything useful, they stayed at home with their mother. But once you could do something, you did it.

As I have said, work filled a lot of our lives. One of the big jobs was looking after the cows. Someone always had to get up in the morning to go to the stables, milk the cows, then go to the dairy to sell the milk. If it was not a school day, you would feed the animals. When you feed them in the morning, it takes hours.

If I was going to school, my father milked the cows, and then he would take the milk to the dairy. When he came home, he used to bring some milk for the children and then we went to school. But if my father had some work, so that he couldn't come home to bring the milk for the children, I had to go there and bring back a litre or a litre and a half in a special flask. Other times I had to take the milk to the dairy to sell and then again I had to bring back some milk for my sisters. Sometimes, we didn't take the milk to sell, but used it to feed the calves, but we still saved some milk for the children.

When you have animals, it is hard work, because they have to be fed twice a day. When the grass was long, it took less time to feed the animals. But sometimes there was not enough grass on our land to feed them. So you went to a different plot – my father had several plots, not just in one place – there were lots of small pieces. That meant you needed to walk a long distance with the grass for the animals. Sometimes it took an hour just to get there and back, not counting the time it took to cut the grass. You cut any grass you could, because nothing was wasted – even if you cut a hedge to clear a path, you used it. When we had planted a crop, for example potatoes or wheat, sometimes there was nothing in those fields to feed the animals, so you had to go to another valley or another hill, where the ground had not been dug. Then I walked back with the grass on my head. It was like that even after I got married.

To cut the grass we had a *foice* (sickle). There were two sorts. One had a saw edge and the other was like a knife, just sharp and smooth. Some grass you could cut with the knife type, but for some you had to use the saw. Sometimes the blades needed to be sharpened. At home we had a *lima* (file) to sharpen the knife type, but for the ones with teeth we needed to go to the *ferreiro* (blacksmith) to make the teeth deep again, because they got worn and blunt when you used the sickle a lot.

Weather and Water

Because Madeira is part of Portugal, and a lot further south, it is easy to think that it is like the Mediterranean there. But we forget that it is an island well out into the Atlantic, and mountainous. So the weather can be cold, wet and violent, even though it can be very hot in summer.

To a farming community, water is especially important, because of the need for irrigation. Maria's account shows that she, for one, is convinced that the weather has changed in the last half-century. This is supported by official Portuguese government figures, which say that since the 1970s the mean temperature in Funchal has increased by about 0.6 C per decade. But Maria is also certain the activity of humans has done irreversible damage to the environment. She tells us that many of the streams she knew as a young woman have vanished.

She also mentions a couple of types of food which may be surprising. One is that they used to catch sea bass, even though they lived inland. This is because it is a species which can tolerate wide changes in the saltiness of water, and so they can move into fresh water.

The other is a seafood delicacy unknown in Britain. Until I met Maria, I thought I was the only Englishman or even the only person in the world who had ever collected and eaten lapas...

We had four seasons then but now it's less so. So the weather changed a lot during the year. We had a long summer – it was hot but it could rain some days. In May, June, July and August it can rain one day and the next day it is hot again. So May was a hot month but it could also rain – I remember we had a saying "*O sol de maio faz os pintos tontos!*" (The May sun makes the chickens go mad!), because it was so hot. And for June we said: "*O mês de São João é mijão*" (St John's month pees a lot!) because June was hot but rainy. It was not heavy rain, but it could damage the fruit

– the grapes and so on. And the wind could tear off the flowers of the fruit trees, which meant that you didn't get fruit.

August is a hot month and September isn't bad. But the first weekend of September it always rains! At that time there is the festival of the Senhor Bom Jesus at the church in Ponta Delgada. I went once with my parents. People make a pilgrimage to pray for a miracle or to give thanks. On that weekend it always rains, but the festival is still always crowded. They used to go in open vans and sang all the way, and they stayed for the whole night, and slept in the vineyards. Because there are the vine leaves, when it rained they stayed dry. Some people brought plastic sheets and hung them from the vines to make a cover while they slept.

Nowadays the weather has changed but before, the winter was real winter. It would rain a lot and so we used to put buckets and any other containers to catch the water as it came off the roof. We did that because it saved us from having to go a long way to get water.

October is not that cold but November, December, January and February are very cold, and very rainy too. It rains more than in other parts of the island and then during the night you felt cold. And it often hails. We didn't get snow, but you could see it on the mountains – everything was covered in white. I never went there, so it was only when I came to England and I saw the trees covered with snow, that I realised what it was really like. A lot of visitors go to the mountains for the snow, but quite a few have died. That's because there are trees and the ground is covered with snow, so it looks like it is flat, but it isn't.

At times in winter it rained and rained, and it was windy. There was thunder and lightning – it was very scary. It seemed to be just overhead and it looked like everything was shaking. So people were very scared and they prayed. They covered electrical equipment when that came to the village, and they disconnected the electricity, because they felt it would connect with the lightning.

I remember one night there was a fire. It was very bad weather – it was pouring with rain – and yet there was a fire in the stable and there was nothing to stop it. It was the lightning that had started it. The fire gave a reflection and we got up in the night to see it. Everyone around could see it because it is not flat country – you can see from a long way off.

One time the ground started shaking – it was an earthquake. It happened during the day at about 11 am. I was in the stable and it was shaking. I was a teenager and I thought it was a young man inside the stable trying to scare me. And on the other side there was a lady – she was screaming because she couldn't keep her balance. But we got my family out of the house – some houses were destroyed. There was a lot of damage in the country.

I have memories of bad winters when there were a lot of avalanches, because it kept on raining, and people died. I remember one time there was a car in the stream and the priest was there. The avalanche rushed through the street and swept up the car and took it on into the water.

In winter people made sure there were ditches to take away the water off the land. In the summer the ditches were dry, but before the winter people made sure they were clear, so they would let the water pass.

In the old days Madeira was rich in springs, but afterwards they built a lot of tunnels through the mountains to take roads and the water drained away, and many streams dried up, so the land became dry. Some streams came straight from the mountains, some from lower down. The ones starting in the mountain always had water. But the very small streams during the summer were dry. Then in winter they get full. So we had to keep the streams and ditches clear, because when it rained, the streams overflowed, the land got covered with a lot of water and the water needed to drain away. Now the weather has changed. So when it rains for a few days, the streams get full and then there is a lot of damage, because they are not kept clear like before.

Near our house we had a stream with rocks and all the way it had water. At that time we washed our clothes in it, because we didn't have washing machines. I remember that when I was young, suddenly the stream got very full, and we had to get out fast, and the water took the clothes. There was no time to clear them away, because in the mountains it had rained a lot and then the water rose suddenly. Sometimes you can see quite clearly that it is raining in the mountains, but because the rain was a long way off, we didn't bother about it. Now they warn people to take care when the weather is like that. So even when they go to wash the clothes, they stay on the side of the stream, because you never know what will happen.

I remember my father and some people knew places in the stream where there was a big, deep dip. In summer they went there, because there was not much water further upstream, but at that place they could take water for the land. It could be so dry that you needed water, even just to make the grass grow.

There were fish in the stream. Always in the middle it was full of water, and my father used to go there with my brother to catch them. I remember one type of fish was very small but very long – in Portuguese we call it *erozes (*eels). The meat is white, but we didn't fancy it. The other fish was sea bass. It is a sea fish, but they found it inland in the stream.

Then there were big tanks next to the mountains, in the foothills, where the water ran all the time, because they were next to the stream. The government looked after the fish – there were thousands there. People went there to see them, and during the night some went there to steal some! That was because in the streams, the fish just came when they did, so some people didn't bother about fishing. My father was different – he was always interested in trying to catch them.

But he didn't go fishing in the sea. He wasn't keen on the sea, and he didn't like us to go there – it was seen as a bit shocking. Perhaps it was because the sea is very rough near us. So people were scared to go swimming, and in our area not many people knew how to swim. In other parts of the island it is different, and people go to swim a lot – for instance, my cousin who lives in Funchal – she loves to swim.

But one thing you could find on the rocks was *lapas* (limpets). When I came to England, I found that people didn't eat them, and some people even thought they were disgusting. But for us they are a nice treat, especially when you pickle them.

O Pão Nosso De Cada Dia Nos Dai Hoje
(Give us this day our daily bread...)

In modern London, and elsewhere, there is a great interest in the cuisine of other countries. This has led to a popular image of Mediterranean cuisine which to us is exotic and exciting. Maria's account shows that, for the most part, gastronomy is a pastime for those with time and/or money to spare.

The ingredients had to be what could be produced locally and by one's own family. Furthermore, others which we now see as normal, such as pasta, sugar or honey, were used sparingly, because they had to be paid for. You had also to decide whether to eat the food you produced food to or to sell it. This was true, for instance, of eggs.

We also think of wine as being freely consumed in Mediterranean countries. But for Maria, there was only the amount of wine you had actually been able to make, so it had to be used wisely. Yet it is clear that hungry workers liked and got full plates, and there were the festivals, when special treats were possible and looked forward to.

One treat which Maria still enjoys has been known for centuries, and was mentioned by the poet Geoffrey Chaucer in his Franklin's Tale*: Wel loved he by the morwe a sop in wyn. (In the morning he really loved a sop in wine).*

Every morning we had breakfast – we had what was left over from the night before. You reheated it, and if it was not enough, you added some water and cut some bread into small pieces and put that into the soup. It was always like that until life got better. During the morning you could eat fruit if you were near the trees and it was the right season.

If people were working for you, different things could happen. They could be working a long way from our house – as far as from Camden Town to Highgate. On those occasions the owner of the land took their breakfast to where they were working.

One thing I remember happily was the fruit. On the edges of the fields there were trees with oranges, peaches, apples and chestnuts. And there was cane sugar – it was so sweet. You didn't have it every day, just in the season, but it was so tasty. You took the skin and squeezed it and sucked – aaah!

At midday it was lunchtime, which was a new, big meal. We just had one thing for lunch. You ate till you were full, and that was it. Normally, those workers who were busy near the house came in and ate with the family. If they were working at a distance, my mum would cook food and take it to them in a large basket. She could do this because very often the meal was vegetables which were boiled and then drained, before they were put on the table in a basket for people to help themselves. Sometimes there might also be a bit of *bacalhau* (dried cod).

In the old days they didn't have many plates. So people had an *alguidare* – a sort of large earthenware bowl in the middle of the table, and you helped yourself. But you didn't take anything from the middle – you had an area on the edge in front of you, where you dipped in. If you were eating *milho (*corn flour), which was quite solid, you made a sort of wall with it in the *alguidare* round your part and you put your food in there. But in my Mum's house I never remember eating in that way – she gave us the food on plates.

But she did use the *alguidare* to serve *sorde*. This is a dish which uses salt, garlic, oil, eggs and *milho,* and bread, cut into small pieces. My mother served it in the *alguidare* but then gave us our portions on plates. Often we ate it with sweet potatoes, which was very good. That certainly made us very full!

We cooked on a wood fire – it makes the food very tasty. We didn't roast the meat – we boiled or fried it. Everyone had a frying pan. My mum had one she brought from Mozambique – it was the sort that lasts for life. The food tasted different because of the material it was made from, which was *ferro* (iron). It was very hard, not like the saucepans you cook in now. But after my mum got a cooker, she got a new pan – the cast iron one was for the wood fire. And I remember that the food never stuck to it – and what you cooked – especially things like fish and eggs – had a crisp outside.

We cooked what we had in storage, things such as dried beans, cornmeal, potatoes, sweet potatoes and yams. To prepare beans, you put them in water the day before, because they were dried. We had potatoes every day. If they were big potatoes, you might cut them in small pieces. But one thing I liked was raw carrots – I still do!

At that time we used a lot of wheat, maize and potatoes in our diet. You couldn't buy a nice meal from the shop – we didn't have many facilities or much choice. It was all home cooking. We sometimes had pasta or rice, but not often because you needed to buy them. In the shop they had a big bag of maybe 20 kilos. No one could afford that, so people just bought a small quantity, maybe half a kilo. It was not like now, in a packet. For instance, with sugar they measured it on the scales and put it in a small bag.

As I say, potatoes were very important to us. We planted them and then put the cow's manure and waste straw and a chemical fertiliser around them. At that time this work was done at the beginning of the year, but now they plant at different times of the year, because the weather has changed. A bit earlier, before Christmas, we also planted onions. You put the seeds in the ground and when the seedlings appear, you thin them out and move the thinned-out plants to another space.

Nowadays, they usually harvest the potatoes a bit later in the summer, at the beginning of autumn, and after that they plant some new ones. But that doesn't yield as well as if you plant at the beginning of the year – they grow smaller and you get a smaller quantity. But many people don't care – they just want some potatoes for home use when the previous crop has been used up. We grew them to live on, though if you planted a lot, you could sell them.

With potatoes, a few weeks after planting you need to put more earth on them to cover them up, otherwise they grow out and they don't grow properly. It took three to four months before you harvested them – we took them up in the summer. As I was the oldest, I had to help the adults in lifting the potatoes, but my sisters had to assist on the land as well.

When you take potatoes, you put the big ones on one side, and you set aside the nice ones for next season. The small ones you leave behind. The children had to pick these – but we hated it! First you pick them and then separate them. The small ones get "eyes" and after a few months they shrink, so my mum always tried to use the small potatoes first.

We preferred to harvest the potatoes when it was good weather and the ground was dry. If it is raining, the mud sticks on them. Then you had to take them and put them inside your house in your cellar. If the wet mud is left on potatoes, they rot. So you leave them in the house to dry and then move them to the store.

As I said before, we kept chickens. Some hens were for kept by people for their eggs and the eggs were for sale. and some people went to the village to buy eggs. For the chickens to lay eggs, you need to feed them better. But my father didn't like to sell the eggs and we saved them in a basket. We didn't usually give them to other people – if you gave eggs to someone, they had to be a very nice person, because there were not enough.

One of our neighbours had a lot of chickens and lots of eggs which she sold. When people came to work for her, she used to beat the eggs into an omelette to give to them, because with an omelette they got more to eat with fewer eggs. And she added water to the mixture to make more of it – she was very mean!

When my mum made food where she needed to boil herbs, sometimes she put in eggs – not many, not one for each child, but she just cut off a bit for the children. Or sometimes after she had put the egg in the saucepan, she would save it and just use it to give a taste to a dish.

To fry an egg was very rare, but when they had people working on the land, the workers had fried bread in a sort of sandwich. It was not like the sandwiches you get here! They made loaves of bread which had two halves. You cut them down the middle, fried an egg and put it between the two halves. The frying fat soaked into the bread. The workmen would eat the whole thing. It may sound a lot, but you have to remember that they worked hard for long days, so they got a big appetite. Nowadays they don't eat a whole loaf of bread, perhaps just four slices. And of course they would have a glass of wine with it!

We had meat sometimes, but not much – we added a bit to give flavour. If you didn't have any meat, you could marinade potatoes in the juice. The meat we had was usually pork. We killed the pig in December and stored most of it. One thing we did was to salt it. We washed it, but even if it was still salty, you ate it – nobody complained.

On Sundays the food was a bit better. We had a stew – you could put a bit of meat in it. But if we didn't have meat, we fried onions in a saucepan, with a bit of oil and paprika, and pureed tomato and let it cook until reduced. Then you add water and potatoes or pasta. If she wanted pureed tomatoes, my mum bought a tin. When she had opened it, you added a little olive oil on to cover the puree. Even if the top got a bit dirty, it lasted for longer – the oil helps to preserve it.

When we had pork meat, we cut it into small pieces and put a marinade with it, made of herbs and wine. We fried it. Another thing we made was *cozido à portuguesa*. You take some meat and boil it with cabbage, potatoes and herbs. You just eat it like that – there is nothing else with it. The cabbage can have a very strong taste, especially if the leaves are old, but it gave taste to the potatoes.

We kept the pork fat for the whole year – we used a lot of fat at that time. For instance, we used it with potatoes because by themselves they were too dry. You can also fry onions cut into small pieces in that fat.

We also ate offal – intestines (chitterlings), tripe, liver and kidneys.

Sometimes we had fish, sometimes mackerel, but especially cod. We didn't live by the sea, but during the season men came to the village to sell fish. On some Sundays, when we left the church, there was a small garden where they sold it, like a market. I remember mackerel, fresh tuna and *pesce espada* (swordfish). My father bought it, then he brought it home and cleaned it. We gave the left-overs from the cleaning to the cats or the dogs.

We always fried the fish (we didn't have an oven or a cooker till later). We used meat fat. We didn't have olive trees in Madeira. But later there was oil, when life was better, and then we didn't want to use the meat fat.

One dish many people now know about was *bacalhao,* which is dried codfish. It was a good thing to have because it lasted longer, as does *choriço*, the Portuguese sausage – we didn't have fridges at that time. You boil it and put it in a bowl with onions, garlic and parsley. That was the only time we used oil, on top of it. You ate it for the main meal, with corn bread. You soaked the bread in the marinade and vinegar, which was not that strong. It comes from wine which has gone sour – you didn't go to a shop to buy it. Another thing was that when you cooked *bacalhau,* the water tasted of fish. So we could add that to a sauce, because it had both salt and the fish taste together – you want something tasty. But I remember that some people were very poor and they didn't even have that.

Sometimes when we didn't have meat or fish, there was just potatoes, boiled potatoes, then you needed something extra to eat. So we just took onions cut into small pieces and put them in a bowl of vinegar, with garlic, parsley and olive oil, and when it is cooked you have that sauce to soak the potatoes in and give them the tastes of the other ingredients. You add a bit of salt – it tastes nice! When you have onions, the sauce can be very strong. If so, you add a bit of water. If there were other people there, though, you were only supposed to dip your potato once.

Milho (cornflour, made from maize) was an important part of our diet. You can just cut it and eat a piece, or you can soak it in sauce. It was very popular, because you grew it on your land. You cooked it at least once a week, and then it lasted for more than one meal. You could fry it and eat it, or you could eat it cold. And you can make food for the animals with it as well.

When you make bread with *milho,* it doesn't last just for two days, like wheat bread – it lasts for two weeks or longer, until it gets mouldy. They baked the bread until it was very brown, because then it lasts much longer. But it's not that soft.

When the *milho* is cold, but you don't want to eat it cold, you can eat it in different ways. One favourite of ours was *sor-de,* which I mentioned earlier. You boil water, then add some herbs, garlic and a bit of oil or fat – mostly at that time it was fat. You can add some eggs if you want. When it is ready, you get a bowl, you cut the *milho* bread into small pieces and put it in the bowl and add the boiling liquid, so that the water heats the *milho.* As the bread gets softer, it soaks up the liquid. If you want it very liquid, you have less bread and if you want it thicker, you add more bread. But you don't want it too thick, because you need the water to eat with the *mihlo.* That's because sometimes the bread is very hard.

When the bread was hard, we would also slice it and fry it. We beat eggs, and soak the sliced bread in the eggs and then fry it with the egg on both sides – then you eat it – mmm!

They fed small babies – maybe after 6 months – with corn meal, ground very fine. They roasted it in the oven, after they made the bread. Then they put it in the milk for the children to start to get solids. At that time the food for children was harder. For babies it's not easy to eat, but as soon as they could eat, you gave them anything you were eating.

At lunch we normally just drank water. You had water to drink because the meal tasted salty and you had to drink a lot of water. And the more you drink, the more full you feel.

Water tasted different in different places – water from a spring was very nice, but some springs were better than others. On our land, even in summer, the spring water was cold, as if it had been chilled in a fridge. We used that water to cook and drink.

I recall that my father made a plastic pipe beside the road to carry water from his land to our house. Only later, after many years the Government laid on piped water. But people were jealous of my father's private supply and they made holes in the pipes. So my father gave up on that.

There was a public fountain near my parents' house. It was a tank which the water filled up, though you didn't see it come in – it got there through a pipe. It's still there and people still like to have water from it.

But on special days we drank coffee afterwards – or you could eat your food with coffee, if you preferred. We got coffee from the shop. They had coffee beans, and they ground them for you. You put the ground coffee into water and boiled it, and then when you poured it, you used a strainer to catch the grounds. But because coffee was expensive for us, we didn't put a lot in the pot, so it was always rather weak – it was still nice though!

We didn't usually have wine – not many people had wine to drink every day. In fact, my father had a vineyard, a big one, so we had wine sometimes during the year, on special days. When we grew up (really, when we were not very old), we started to drink wine with my parents. Now they don't give alcohol to children, because it is bad for them, but at that time they didn't know. Of course they didn't give much to the children.

But wine was always available. My father put a tap on the barrel and you could take some when you wanted. I remember that when there were several people, there was a 250ml aluminium jug we used to catch the wine and pour it out for them.

But it wasn't that people drank wine all the time, like in a pub – it was just there, part of life. And it was the custom to offer visitors a glass. I remember that the first thing my grandmother did when visitors came was to offer them a glass of wine.

And if people were working for you, you provided wine. And they had a lot of wine! If the employer didn't have their own supply, they had to buy it to take to the land for the people who were working there.

Sometimes, you would use the wine like a meal – I still do it now, once in a while, when it is very cold. You put sugar in a glass or a cup, and then the wine to make it sweet. Then you soak bread in it. Wine takes more sugar than coffee, and when it is sweet, it is nice to drink – but you get drunk easily. Perhaps it's because you tend to drink a lot more when it's sweet!

We sometimes had another drink, using milk. They boiled milk and put mint in it and then drank it in a cup or in a bowl. They had it with hard bread – hard, because soft bread would melt – and often they ate it for breakfast. But I never drank it, because I didn't like milk – like I said before, it was because I was used to condensed milk in Mozambique. When I came to England, I started slowly to drink normal milk.

If you had people working for you, you gave them another meal in mid-afternoon. But that was much lighter, some bread, and wine or coffee, and the food left over from lunch. That was only in summer, when the days were long.

In the evening when you came home, you had a fresh meal. And any people working for you had to come home and have some.

Every night we had soup – a meal you ate with a spoon, not a knife and fork – knives and forks were for Christmas and for special events in our tradition. Everyone ate soup. You can put a lot of things together and it is easier to feed the family.

For instance, we used to have pumpkin soup. There were different types of pumpkin – there was *abobra* and *buganga*. When it grew, we would pick some young – and you can eat it like that. But we let a lot grow and they get harder and more dry. Then you harvest the pumpkins and put them in storage, and you can eat them months after. You took the skin off and cooked what is inside. And another good thing was the seeds. They were wet when you took them out, so you put them in the frying pan – that dried them and they were a lovely snack – like having nuts or crisps.

To make a soup you often added cabbage and watercress – at that time, there were a lot of streams where it grew. Now you don't find it wild and they plant it. But at that time it was fresh – you could go anywhere and come to a stream with cress growing in it. There was one at the edge of our land and my mother used to go and collect some, and keep it in water to keep it fresh, if she wanted to cook it the next day.

We had just one course in the evening. If you cooked sweet potatoes or *milho* for lunch and there was some was left over, in the evening you ate it with a sauce. When you cooked sweet potatoes, you put them on the grill over the fire. The skin got burned, but the inside got warm and you could eat it. After that you could keep them in a basket for the next day.

Bread and Wine

Maria describes the harvesting and milling of wheat. She takes for granted knowledge which many of us no longer have, so it may be helpful to read the simple account given on page 143.

Once again, procedures in the wider world were very different. As early as 1835, in the United States, Hiram Moore had built the first combine harvester, a machine which can reap, thresh and winnow grain. By the time Maria was born these machines were huge, highly efficient and, of course, driven by motors. However, we should perhaps temper any sense of superiority over the simpler processes of Maria's youth, since combine harvesters generate heat, meaning that the dry cereal products can easily catch fire – in the final fifteen years of the last century, there were nearly 700 such fires in the United States alone.

Maria also mentions the chore of grinding grain to produce flour, using a hand mill (a quern). Again, we can see the amazing continuity of traditions which Maria experienced – the use of querns is known to date from the Neolithic period.

Wheat was very important, because it gave us flour to make bread.

First you had to dig the soil. The method was different from that for potatoes – we didn't add the fertiliser. We planted the seeds and then three months later, we got a lot of people working in a line to take out the weeds. Then you left it to grow through July and August. We didn't water it. When harvest time came we hoped for good weather, and that it would not rain, because it has to be dry when you harvest it.

In Britain you cut the wheat, but we didn't. We held it by the stalks and we pulled it from the ground. Then we laid it down on the ground and tied it into bundles. We cut off the heads to take to the threshing machine. But there was always some left behind, and the children had to do the gleaning – I felt they were like chickens picking up the seeds – though they didn't eat them of course!

The stalks were left to let them dry, and become straw. Then you could use it for so many things – to put in the stable under the cows to make the ground warm, and for thatching the roofs. Once the cows' straw had their manure on it, you put it onto the fields and dug it in.

To get the wheat grains they used a machine – there was one person in the area who had one. They put it near the edge of our land, because we had no proper roads. So you had to carry the wheat to it, and put it into the machine. There was one man there, the engineer, but all the people had to work together to do the work.

There were in fact two machines. One was to get the seeds – to separate the wheat from the chaff, and the other was used to pass the seeds again to make them cleaner, because there were still the husks on them.

Everything was done by hand. Everybody, both men and women, had to help. The first machine had the engineer, the other worked by hand. You put a cloth on the ground, rather like a doormat. It was linen, like you used for bedspreads. You put it on the ground so you didn't lose any seeds. When we had finished with the machine, we took the grain home and put it into *sacos de lona* (canvas sacks, made of hemp). They lasted a long time and you could wash them and use them again.

If it had been wet weather, you had to put the wheat to dry outside your house, and it dried for a few days. But if it rained, you had to bring it in and wait until the weather was good. Then you had to put it out again.

After it was dry, you put it in a big box made of wood. There was one for the corn and one for the wheat, though sometimes you had a box divided in the middle. This kept the grain in a good condition – but you had to be careful to keep it dry all the time.

When the grain was ready, we took it to the mill, when we wanted flour. You didn't go to the mill just once – you went there often, just with the amount you wanted to use. On Porto Santo they had windmills all over the island, but on Madeira, because we were rich in water, we had water mills.

When you got there, but before it went into the machine, it was measured. At that time we didn't measure in kilos. Instead we measured with two boxes. One box they called an *alqueiro* and the other one, which was smaller was called *uma quarta* (one quarter), because four measures from that filled the big one.

When the mill was ready for you to use, you measured it again, and the miller, a woman, took some – that was the way you paid. In fact it was the same with the threshing machine. We measured the seeds, and maybe you had five *alqueiros* for us and one for him – I don't remember exactly. Nowadays we still have the water mill, but the people there don't want the grain – they are paid money.

At the mill they separate out the fine flour and the rough (wholemeal) flour and the bran, which was very rough. When we brought the flour home, we kept it in a linen bag. When you went to the mill, it produced both fine and rough flour. The rough we cooked and we made soup with it, but even when it was cooked, it was a bit rough. We didn't waste the bran – we gave it to the pigs or chickens, though sometimes in winter, in January, February and March, when we didn't have much produce from the land, we used the bran as well.

To make the flour we used a hand mill – a quern. It had a stone, with another stone on top, and there was a handle to move it around. In the middle of the top stone there was a hole. You put the seeds in there slowly, and you moved the top stone round – slowly because you couldn't move it fast – it was very hard work. My father wanted my mum to use it, because his parents did, but she made everyone take a turn!

With *milho* we had a simple machine the *maquina de esbagoar* (corn stripper). You fed in one corn cob at a time, while someone turned the handle. The seed came out of the bottom. You have to remember that this works because when you cut the *milho*, the seeds are not soft, like you buy in a supermarket, but hard. So the machine can shake them or knock them off.

As well as growing wheat and corn for food, we grew grapes and made our own wine. We used to spray the vines before the grapes grew, and we used the same thing for the potato leaves. This is to stop them getting burned. If the leaves burn, the grapes die. This can happen when there are clouds, and especially when it is foggy. It is very bad for the crops, if it comes from the north, from the sea.

There was a substance – we called *ameixa*. You can get it as a yellow powder. They used to put it on the grapes. My uncle used it, because he got a lot of grapes and his wine was very strong. But not everyone used it. My father never put it in his vineyard, so his wine was weaker, but it was more healthy and not chemical.

When the grapes were ripe, we cut them with a small knife, when they were ready – nowadays they have a special tool. We put them in small wicker baskets and when they were full the children carried them to the edge of the vineyard, where they put them into big baskets. We had to carry these to another place to press the grapes, because there were no cars.

Some people had a place to press the wine, but the ones that didn't have one used other people's, and they weren't charged for it. My grandfather had a place of his own, and at first we didn't. But later my father made one for himself. It was a sort of tank made of cement.

They made the wine in September. It had to be left for a time, while it fermented – I remember it seemed to boil, like water.

There were two tanks – a big one and a small one. They put the grapes in the big one. Then we squeezed the grapes by walking on them. You had bare feet, no boots (nowadays they do have boots). If you had boots on, you had to take them off and roll your trousers up, because there was a big quantity of grapes.

If you kept on your boots the people said "Oh, the wine smells bad!" Sometimes they said that it smelled because of the smell of the feet – they didn't wash their feet! Your feet and hands went red because of the grapes, and it took a while for it to wear off. Or they could even be black – it depended on the type of grape, because some have a very strong colour.

At that time just men did it – there were a lot of men around and it was seen as a man's job, but now it's mixed. In fact, when they worked with the wine, even if the wine was in a barrel ready to take it out, if a woman had a period, they didn't go to the wine press or touch the wine, because people believed it changed the quality. I think it did, that something changed. But the women didn't say they had a period, because we didn't talk about those things at that time – they were embarrassed. They just said they wouldn't go there.

As they squeezed the wine in the big tank, it came to a small outlet to pass into the small tank. They used to put a wicker basket outside the big tank over the hole, so the loose grapes didn't get into the wine. Then they took the wine from the small tank and put it into a barrel.

If the wine was pressed in your house, there was no problem. But if not, you had to carry it in a pot or a small bag that held 50 litres. The men carried the bags on their shoulders and the girls carried small pots – I remember doing that.

They made the bag in a traditional way. They took the skin of a goat. They cut off the neck and the legs, and they peeled it off the animal. Then they let it dry – I don't know if they treated it. They made this into a bag to carry wine – about 50 litres. We called it a *burracho*. They filled it with wine but it was soft skin on their shoulders, so it didn't hurt you even though it was heavy. If you carry a barrel, you have 50 litres and the weight of the barrel, so they preferred the goat skin.

When they made the wine, they used to work with the moon. That was also important when you planted crops. I don't know why, but if you plant things with the right moon, they grow quickly. But if the moon is lower, the plants come out unevenly or some don't grow at all. The important times were the new moon and the full moon. They didn't plant at night, but it was at that time of month.

The same was true when you made wine. When you made wine at the right time, it would ferment fast and come out of the barrel, like when you boil water. If the moon is lower, the wine takes longer to ferment or doesn't come up to the top of the barrel. So you didn't fill the barrel – you needed to leave a gap. They would put a stick inside and measure how much was there.

The wine doesn't ferment on the same day you put it in the barrel – it takes a day or so to settle down. Then it boils every day and night. So you just put it in the barrel and leave the top open, because if you cover the barrel, it will spoil – you need to leave it open. You wait until it has settled down. You can hear when it has stopped fermenting, but you need to put your ear next to the barrel. Then after a few weeks you cover it.

Before you fill the barrel, it has to be cleaned. So they wash the barrel, but often it is still not really clean. So they tested it with a substance we called *ameixa*.

This *ameixa* came in a little strip, rather like chewing gum. You fix it inside the barrel and then you light it. It makes a very small flame, almost no flame, just shouldering like the fuse of a firework. Then you cover the top, because the smell and fumes are very bad for you. When it is alight, it drips like a candle, so you have to be careful not to use too much, otherwise the wine gets the taste.

Like I said, it smells and the fumes make you cough. And I remember that one day they had an argument in the corner shop – they were open in the evening, because it was a *taverna* for the men at that time. So someone put *ameixa* under the door, and they all started coughing and rushed out!

They kept the wine in the barrel when it was done, until 11 November when they had a festival – it was called São Martinho.

They used to taste the wine on that day – it was always then – it didn't matter what the moon was.

After that, they liked to move the wine to other containers to get the waste to make *aguardente*. Next they washed the barrel properly and they put something inside to check it was clean. Then they put the wine back. If they didn't take out the dregs in November, they could do it later, but then they checked the moon to decide when they should do it.

To make *aguardente,* you use a special pot – the still – which is handmade. They put wood underneath and make a fire, but it has to be a very low flame. The liquid boils and the steam comes out and passes into another pot. There is very little of it and it comes out like water. You can drink it, but it is very rough, so they like to boil it again, to make it smoother. They can divide it into rough and smooth, but I don't know how. But when it is good, it gives less, and some people want quantity, so they take the rough spirit. My grandfather and father both made *aguardente*, and my sister still takes the dregs of her wine to a person who makes it that way.

Children's Games and Stories

For younger people it is very difficult to imagine entertainment without video games. These had first been developed as early as 1950, but were prohibitively expensive, and so could not be part of the life of the ordinary person. But the rapid growth in computer power, and steeply falling prices meant that a form of ping-pong game, called Pong, *appeared in 1972. Six years later, when Maria was becoming a young woman and already married, the Japanese company Taito released* Space Invaders, *which many people would say was the true beginning of the demand for video games.*

Maria's account of children's pastimes could not be more different from the experience of many readers. This was partly because in Maria's society children did not have a lot of spare time. As we have already seen, they were needed to help with the work of the farm and the household chores.

But for many of us, the most notable difference will be the absence of books. This was partly a question of cost, but more fundamentally, there could be no reading of stories to children, because few of the adults could read. In 1950 75% of the population were still illiterate.

Nevertheless, the reader will recognise the children's games, as well as their perennial interest in things that are scary.

We didn't have much time to play with other children, even though at that time children were not involved much with adults. I remember that if women were talking and a child was around, they made us go away, so we wouldn't hear the adults' conversation. This was true, even if it was things we needed to know about, such as women's periods. Your friends and people you knew at school or at work told you – but you didn't get it from adults. Maybe, they were kind of ashamed or something – I don't know exactly.

But when we did play, I remember we had a skipping rope, and we played *as escondidas* (hide and seek) when we were small.

And sometimes my mum would cook a pumpkin. Normally you gave the skin to the pigs, but you could make a design with the skin. So my mum would cut it with a knife, and make a person.

Boys and girls were separate in many ways. As children, the girls played girls' games and the boys played their own games – they certainly didn't play girls' games! And they never wore pink!

I didn't have stories read from a book, I just had books from school, but nobody could read them to me. But I remember they kept telling stories from memory, and of course you listened to them. Some of them were true – or said to be – stories about things that had happened to people, for example stories about when a person made a mistake in the way they talked.

I remember one story well. It shows how if you wanted to give an example to the children, you could tell a story.

At Easter time on Fridays, we don't eat meat. Even if you eat meat by mistake on those days, you have to go to the church and pray. So to show the children that you don't eat meat on those days, and that if you do, God can punish you, we had a story – we were told it was a true story.

There was a man whose wife didn't want to cook meat on Good Friday. But he insisted and he said "I can eat meat if I want." Well, when he started to eat the meat, it stuck in his throat and he passed away. I always remember that story.

Some stories were told to scare the children – and they could scare adults too. We didn't have electricity and everything was very dark at night. Sometimes when you walked outside, you couldn't see anything – you just guessed, because you knew the way. Well, there were people who liked to scare anyone who was out walking. They made noises, or whistled, and sometimes they put on something white, such as a sheet. Other times they kept quiet, and when someone passed, they would take a hard pumpkin and throw it on the ground, and then, because it's steep wherever you go, the pumpkin rolls and makes a noise.

In the countryside, you have trees and wind, and it can sound a bit scary anyway, and then the more you are scared, and the more you hear the funny noises, the more you think "It's real, what they say." If a person was scared, the noises made their fear worse. So some people didn't want to go out at all at night.

Another thing I remember was not a story, but something we said. We talked about one bird, the *coruja* (owl) that sings at night. When people heard it, they thought someone was going to die. But we also had a saying *"Como as corujas, andão de noite"* (Like the owls, they go about at night). We said that about people who went out at night – for example people who were going to commit a crime – or there was one woman, her husband had died, and she had a lot of affairs, but she went to meet the men at night, so people would not see her.

I do remember one story about a dog with a piece of meat. He was by a river, and he saw a shadow pass on the water of the river – it was a piece of meat – of course it was really the reflection of his own piece. It looked better, so he dropped the one he had and jumped into the water to get the other piece!

I think there were rhymes, but I don't remember them. And they sang to babies when they were crying. In our family I was the oldest, so I remember doing that with my sisters. The trouble was that when one cried, the others cried too. They always did the same as each other!

When we did have the chance to play, we often played skipping. We counted when we did it. I wasn't good at that because I was tall, and I always lost. I think it wasn't my fault – it was because the others were smaller than me and couldn't swing the rope high enough.

Another game was when we joined hands and made an arch. I don't remember what they said. They used to pass underneath and around and each time there was no place for one person.

We also played *as escondinhas* (hide and seek) We used to count up to 31 for the people to go and hide. But when you counted, you tried to look! The others hid a long way off and you had to go and find them. But they were clever and you didn't hear anything and you walked past. Then when you went farther off, they ran back to the wall.

We had another game where you walk in a row faster and faster and we said: *Atrás, atrás passearás/ quem é ultima fica atrás* (Behind, behind you will walk, whoever is last stays behind). When they said the words *quem é ultima fica atrás,* we made a circle. You tried not to be last, before they made the circle, but of course someone always was. Really, we made a game with anything.

Teenage Years

Over the past eighty years or so, possibly no change in the structure of society and social relations has been more marked than the position and expectations of young people between the ages of about 12 to 25. In the United States, a youth culture emerged in the 1930s. As the Great Depression lifted, teenagers would flock to ballrooms, to meet, to show off the latest fashions and to dance to the music of bands such as Benny Goodman.

In Britain these changes began after World War II. Older readers will remember – may even have been – Teddy Boys in the 1950s.

During the first twenty years of Maria's life, young people in Britain turned in large numbers first to the hippie culture, and then to identifying as mods, rockers and punks.

Maria's account of her teen years, after leaving school, once again tells of a life very different. Life was dominated by work. Pleasures were few and simple.

One thing she enjoyed was going to see local women preparing wool to be made into yarn. Again her description reflects thousands of years of tradition. Sheep are sheared in the spring, and their fleeces are "skirted" (which means removing low-quality, very dirty wool, vegetation and dung).

Fleeces are very dirty and they also contain a lot of grease (lanolin). The women then "carded" the ends. This technique opens up any tangles, so that a lot of dirt falls out. It also picks out short bits of wool that are taken up when the shearer has to go over an area twice. These can cause a problem, when you want to spin a very fine yarn. "Carding" makes the fibres lie in parallel, ready for spinning, and uses a special tool known as a carder. This was originally done by using the teasel plant, which has close-set, short spikes.

I left school in the summer before my fourteenth birthday. As soon as I left school, I worked on the farm, with the same responsibilities as an adult. This was because my father went to

Jersey for a few years, working in a hotel as a kitchen porter. He wasn't there all the time, just for a season – they went at Easter and came back home in October – they went just for the summer. They didn't stay in Jersey for the whole year, because they had to leave before a year was up – they just went on a contract. So my father was at home for some months of the year.

But when he was away, the farm work was done by me, my brother (he was two years younger than me), and my mother. She had always been at home before, but at that time, when my father was away, she spent time on the land and worked with us.

I had the responsibility for feeding the animals and milking the cows. I spent all day working on our land or working for other people to get paid. Nothing was complicated, we just did it: it was normal. I was a strong girl and I was healthy and I was big – I wasn't fat though – and because I was big, they took me for a greater age than I was – when I was 16, they thought I was 18. I would work any time, because it was easy to work on the land – you could work for someone or someone worked for you. For instance, you might get someone to dig the ground. My mum paid men to do that.

I remember one man who came to work: he would come for a day and two women had to work a day each to pay him back. I remember they used to say "*Um homem vale por duas mulheres*" (A man is worth two women)! But this suited us. Sometimes, when my father wasn't in Madeira, I went with my mum to do the work, but most of the time I paid the man back by working on my own for two days.

It was hard work but enjoyable, because there were no worries. I got up in the morning, and milked and fed the cows before I went to work for someone else for the day.

Though there was a lot of work, I still feel it was a better life. We didn't have the pressure that you have do the work in a set time. If you didn't finish the work that day, you did it the next day – you could just get up early in the morning to finish it. Yes, you felt tired at the end of the day, but you had no worries on your mind. You slept and the next day you were fresh again. Now people have too much pressure and stress and it's "Don't do this" and "Don't do that" and people say things about you and are more interfering. But there is more freedom now, and people can go out of the country at any time.

In the summer some people did their work at night, when the moon was up, because they wanted to finish the work. But they sang, and because Madeira has hills, you could hear the voices far away. You could know from the voice who was there and who was not, even though you couldn't see them. And when you are young, you like that – you want to be with them. So they gave us drinks and some food and we talked very loud on those nights – it was enjoyable.

In winter, some people worked at night as well. For instance, when they were treating sheep's wool, they had to wash it, and then to open it out and twist it, before they could make the cloth. That kind of job was done by adults who already knew how, not by children. The work was mostly done at night.

I remember I went with my cousin to see it. My father never liked us to work or go out at night – but at that time he was abroad! The sitting room was full of ladies sitting around a small light, it was a paraffin light that gave no more light than a candle. But the people did the work from memory.

The girls I knew were more like workmates rather than friends. I was always very shy, keeping things to myself and at school I was very tall in the class, the tallest, and so I always was put at the back of the classroom.

I don't remember the last day I was at school, but before, in the last year, we went from the village to the town to have extra lessons, and on the way home with my other schoolmates, we used to sit down on the side of the street on the way home, and sit in a group talking – I don't recall what about. That year we spent a lot of time together. But the other children decided everything – they made the plans, or said "Let's go this way" – I never made the decisions. When I left school, it was in June, and my birthday was in October, when I would be 14 years old.

I had a cousin I was friends with, but I couldn't tell her my secrets. And there were neighbours I was friends with, but again I kept my confidences to myself. There was another friend – we liked each other and we teased each other, but still I didn't tell my confidences – I never had a best friend in that way.

Like other young people, I had things I wanted to do – to sew, to travel and to sing. I learned some sewing before I got married, and I have travelled a bit – but I never sing to an audience because I don't have the voice.

At the weekends, Saturday was a day when we mostly worked on the land. We fed the animals and we tried if possible to get some grass ready for them for the next day. For the whole week we worked on the land, but some Saturdays we did cleaning at home, especially when it was sunny and warm; we liked to wash all the bedclothes and so on.

We also prepared for Sunday, because on Sunday we did little or no work. The animals had to be fed, but on Sundays we tried to feed them the easy way, so we had time to rest and go to church in the morning. When you came home, you had lunch, and then you could be with your friends in the village. And in the afternoon you went to the fields again to see to the animals. Sunday was a relaxed day, an easy day.

Another thing was that in those days you didn't have a lot of clothes, as you can nowadays. You had one set of clothes for Sunday to go to church, and another to work in. A lot of people were very poor, so they used to put patches on their clothes – you never get that now.

Really, I didn't spend much time with other young people, but there were times when we met. One was on Sunday. When you went to church, you went in a hurry, but after church you came home in a group, walking slowly and talking, and also you chose your group. After we got home and had eaten something, we would stay around and talk.

There was a social life for young people, but it was different from now. There were no clubs or discotheques or things like that. You had nowhere to go – just the church on Sunday. But when you worked on a farm, they sang and told stories and jokes and laughed and shouted to each other and carried on working. We would sing loud and make life happy. When you work together, you do that.

Another time we met was in the evening during the week. At that time, when we came from another area, on the way home we waited for each other, and stopped and talked in the street, until we got home. Then we would stop and talk outside the door before we went in – not about anything serious – just making life happy – that was wonderful.

Church

Maria has already mentioned going to church and the important days in the year, which were all religious occasions. Here she gives more detail of people's everyday experience of the Church.

The difference between her community and Britain at that time is again extremely marked. For decades Britain has become increasingly secular. In the year of Maria's birth 15 million British people, about one third of the population, were regular churchgoers or claimed a religious affiliation. During the first ten years of her life, this figure fell by 2 million.

But for Maria, the faith of the community was unquestioning, and there was no complex theology, such as was beginning to emerge in the 1960s. Religion was a natural part of everyday life that could provide times of beauty, and comfort in bereavement. Maria and all the community were Roman Catholics. This was a very conservative area, so other religions were not practiced. Consequently, important points in Maria's life were the First Holy Communion, Confession and Confirmation.

Yet we hear that older beliefs persisted which were not always in harmony with Catholic teaching. Some people had no doubt that the dead who were not at peace could appear to their relations. They also believed that wandering spirits went away when it became light, another example of knowledge and beliefs which would have been familiar to her (and our) ancestors, centuries before. Interestingly, the broom superstition she describes is still well known in Hispanic countries and in Brazil. The regular version nowadays is that it is a way to get rid of unwanted visitors – but in Maria's version the visitors are not just an inconvenience...

Our church was (and still is) Roman Catholic – I didn't know any other religion but Catholic. It was very big and in the old style – not like now, when they make a church like a house. It was in the Italian style, very big and beautiful. All the churches were more or less the same size. In the church there were pictures and statues.

The service was in Portuguese, but it used to be in Latin. My mum had a book in Latin and they still say some words in that language.

In church you had to cover your head – but not your face. So some women wore a head scarf – I remember that if people had been in another country, they would bring a present of a scarf. But that was more for the old ladies. We young women wore a veil, in black or white net. Black was usually worn by older women, and white by the young ones.

We didn't normally buy and light candles for ourselves in our church. They did have candles and they lit them to Christ and Mary – but we didn't usually buy candles. In July, on the feast of Santa Ana we went in a procession, and then some people carried big candles that belonged to the church. But at times some people bought and lit a candle to give thanks or to pray for something – to have a baby, or to get well. Often they made a *promessa* (a vow) to God to do something if their prayer was granted.

Every Sunday there was the Offertory. Sometimes they asked for a donation for the candles or for charity, but sometimes they didn't say what the money would be used for. So I don't know exactly what they did with it.

You also paid the priest in cash for some things, for example to carry out a marriage or a baptism.

Or you could go to the priest and pay him to pray for you. Like when my brother-in-law passed away, my aunt went to the church and paid for a mass in his name. Or it could be for an anniversary, things like that. Another thing was that at the start of a mass and in the middle, the priest would read out the names of people we should pray for – there could be five or ten names.

At that time women had their babies at home. After the child was born, they were baptised quickly – certainly within a month. The godparents, the midwife and the father took the baby to the church. The mother didn't go to the baptism, because she was not yet fit. Now they have a meeting for the parents and godparents before the baptism, and they all go – the mother as well.

But sometimes there was a huge worry that the baby could die. So if the baby was not well, they called the priest quickly to baptise it. If the baby died at the time it was born, the midwife used any water she could find and blessed the child in the name of God, so that it would be baptised before it died. If they die before they are baptised, somehow it's not the same child – I don't how to explain it – something is missing there.

Sometimes of course a baby was premature and was stillborn. That is always very sad, and I remember that they did not have a funeral like you had with a baby that had lived. I don't know what they did with the body.

Everyone had First Holy Communion and Confirmation. When you are about seven, you have your First Holy Communion and when you are about fourteen, you have Confirmation. If you got married, you needed to have those sacraments. But in the old days you didn't take the children to the church until just before they prepared for the First Holy Communion. I think it was because they didn't have the clothes and the shoes. Now it is different – you take your child everywhere.

The First Holy Communion happens in the summer, in June or something like that. When I did it, we children prepared for the whole year. Before you went to First Holy Communion, there were ladies who did volunteer work and who taught the children, even though they did not yet go to the church. The ladies gave classes before the mass on Sunday, or after the mass on Saturday afternoon. It's called *catecismo* (catechism). In fact, they still do it.

You had classes for Confirmation, too. To get married or to be a godparent, you have to have done this. And you had to go to all the classes – if you missed, you had to wait until the next year. Your parents didn't like it when that happened – it was a sort of shame. So some parents would appeal to the Bishop. Sometimes, if they had a good reason, he allowed it.

I don't think we learned the Lord's Prayer at school, but we did with the *catecista* and also the *Ave Maria* – you had to learn that. I had a book with pictures and the prayers and at the end of the book there were the Ten Commandments, and for Confirmation you had the *Credo* as well.

When you got close to the First Holy Communion, you went to the church and the priest taught you how you had to sit down, when you had to bend your knee and so on, and what to do when the bread was there. They gave us bread (not the one that was blessed) to teach us how to take it. Then when it was our local festival, the children who had taken their First Holy Communion in that year went in their white clothes in a procession. Also every child gets a rosary at the First Holy Communion. I had a rosary but I was very lazy – I said my short prayers, but the rosary was too long! After that, you have to go to church every Sunday.

When you have your first Holy Communion, you have a first Confession to prepare for it, and after that you have got to go to Confession. For Lent the priest invited other priests to come to the church to hear Confession, and in the week before Easter Sunday there was Confession on one day for women and on another day for men. Almost all the people went. At Easter you have to go and so people left a free day to go. In July you might take it for the Feast of Santa Ana, and you also go to Confession at Christmas. So you go at least three times a year.

Nowadays the priest can sit face to face with you, but then we had the confessional. There was one priest – we knew him because he was from Santana – people were shy of going to him, because they didn't want to face him. Some priests gave advice, but some were bored and just said "In the name of the father" and told you to say three Hail Marys or something like that. So when the people came, they would ask who was there. And sometimes someone would say "He's not good."

So people would swop places in the queue, if they really wanted some advice!

After you went to Confession, you didn't leave it too long before the next time, because you felt guilty – maybe because you had used swear words, or you were aggressive to someone – and then you gave up going to take Holy Communion until you had been to Confession. But now people don't follow those rules. I remember I went to a church in Camden Town recently, and the priests didn't have time for all of us. So they said that they would give a blessing to the people that had not been to Confession, and then they could come to take Holy Communion. We have a prayer you say before you go to take it – you don't have to say it out loud, but you ask God for forgiveness and we had to do that. But some people didn't accept it, because they felt they had not had a proper Confession.

If you are divorced, you aren't supposed to take Holy Communion, but I asked the priest about it, and the priest said I could carry on taking the sacrament, because I wasn't living with someone else. If a woman had been with another man – had had an affair – the priest didn't give her Holy Communion. I remember one lady, she had had an affair, and she was in the queue. But when it was her turn, the priest spoke to her in a low voice, and she walked away without taking it. It was very embarrassing for her, because people were watching and whispered to each other.

After Ash Wednesday, every Friday in the evening until Easter they did the Stations of the Cross. A priest went with them. A man took the cross and the people prayed in front of the statues. They stopped in front of each one and bent and prayed. The men took the cross and the children took the candles, but now it is women who do it.

The priest lived in a house next to the church. Now he lives alone and he has a housekeeper. Before they had a *criada,* just a domestic servant, not someone in the Church. Sometimes she became more than a servant – then we called her the *criada do padre* – it happens.

At that time the priests wore a long black gown everywhere they went. And they had a special hat. Sometimes the priest went to a house, if someone was ill, and then he wore the hat and said prayers. One day my sister ran away when she saw the priest! She almost never went to church, so she was scared of him, because he was walking along a very narrow passage and wearing his black gown and hat. Later they wore a dark suit, but with their special white collar.

We also had nuns. They had a school next to the church, and people liked to put children into it, because they taught more religion. It was called the *escola das irmães* (The School of the Sisters). They still do it. I didn't go there – there was no special reason – the school was not big enough, so they didn't take everyone.

The nuns had a house they lived in, and there they did nursing. If you had a pain or you fell, you went there and they treated you, because there wasn't a clinic in the village. There were also nurses there. It was free. They would give you treatment or an injection. That was because there was no GP in the village – in fact there was only one for the whole huge area.

One man used to do work in the church, like ringing the bells, for example, when someone passed away. They rang with a different sound, and people knew that someone had died. Then he passed away and his children took over. When a child was baptised, the parents gave some money to him. He was called the *sacristão* (the sexton) – and I remember we used to refer to people in the family with that name, instead of their normal family name – for instance Maria *Sacristão* and Pedro *Sacristão*.

When they celebrate the mass, there are two boys who stand by the priest. Sometimes they were they were just local boys, but some of them were studying in a college to become a priest. Some boys went there to study, because it was much cheaper and then, when the time came to decide about entering the Church, they got out!

There were some important things we believed about when people died. We said that people would meet again in Heaven.

And when mothers had lost small children, we said the children were angels, because they were innocent and hadn't committed any sins. People believed those angel children prayed for the family, and people would often pray to them for help when they had a problem.

When you die, your sons and your family pray for you, sometimes for a long time after. For instance, my auntie lost her father when she was very small. She is now 72 and she still talks about him and prays for him all the time and she still says her father looks after her.

When we prayed for people after death, we prayed for them to go to *Purgatorio* (Purgatory) and after to *o Ceu* (Heaven). We prayed for them so they could to go to Heaven more quickly. But people said that if you were bad, you didn't go to P*urgatorio*, you went to the other place – *Inferno*! Some people believed that if you carried on praying for a person like that, because they would never go to Heaven, they didn't want the prayers, and in fact they got more problems. In fact some of the old-fashioned people still believe that when a person doesn't need the prayers, those who are praying hear noises. They say the dead person is asking them to stop praying for them, because it torments them.

Another thing was that some people heard noises, and sometimes they had a vision of a person who had died. They used to say that the noise only happened at night, and stopped when the cock first crew and it began to get light.

Other people might have a dream. Then they said that person had a debt and had come to alert the family to pay that debt. For example, it might be to pay for olive oil, because they had promised to give olive oil to the church – it was lit with olive oil lamps and not candles in the old days. So the family needed to go to the church and pay that debt.

I'm not sure how much of this I believe. I do remember an experience I had, though. My husband had a friend. He was a good, quiet and gentle man, and in fact that meant that all the girls wanted him! But sadly, he had a car accident and was killed. That was on February 2nd.

Well, the following year on 2 February – the anniversary of the accident – we heard a lot of noise in the house during the night. We couldn't sleep, and I must admit we were scared. So I went outside. It was a moonlight night, so it was bright. I could hear the noise but there was nothing there. Nothing was broken. Then I really got scared!

We talked about it and we felt something was wrong. It happened for a few nights. So I went to church and talked to the priest, and paid for a mass to give the man peace. Then the priest came to my house and sprinkled Holy Water to bless it. I don't know if it was all real or true, but the noise did stop.

I did think afterwards that our house was built in terraces and on top we had a clothes line. That made a noise when the wind blew. And the noise I heard was a bit like what you hear on boats when the rigging rattles. But then it had never done that before, and didn't after. So I don't know what I believe.

Another thing was that most people believed in black magic. For example, they were convinced that some women were *feiticeiras* or *bruxas* (witches) who were definitely evil, and if you annoyed them, bad things would happen to you. I remember one woman – her whole family was bad – and everyone was scared of them. Certainly, my uncle believed that she had evil powers, because he had a dispute with her about a right of way, and he then had some bad experiences. He always blamed her.

And lots of people left a broom, standing upside down, with the bristles at the top, behind the front door. This was because they believed that it stopped the *bruxa* from coming in.

Festivals

In a society where people have to work hard, festivals and holidays are very much looked forward to. The events Maria describes are all based on important events in the church year. So it was expected that you would go to church on such days.

For many people these days these feast days are another world. This is especially true of Easter, which is now for many people just an excuse for eating a lot of chocolate – whereas Maria says "Good Friday was the biggest day of the year."

Certain festivals were very much linked with everyday life. So the Feast of São João (St John) whose symbol is a lamb, was the occasion for a sheep-centred festival in the mountains, and to celebrate São Pedro (St Peter) (who in the Bible is described as a fisherman and a "fisher of men") they went to the sea.

*Maria refers to April 1 as "*dia das petas*", which means the day of lies or deceits. It is believed that the tradition of playing tricks dates from the 16th Century in France, when the calendar was changed. The New Year had previously begun on April 1, but was then decreed to start on January 1. There were many who resented the change and continued to follow the old system. They were mocked by those who accepted the new date and were, for example, invited to non-existent celebrations.*

The Festival of the Seven Saints on August 15th is another ancient festival. Maria mentions that the saints being venerated were all women. This was because for the Catholic Church it is the commemoration of the Assumption of the Virgin Mary – the day on which, after her death, her body was taken up directly into Heaven. So these are locations dedicated to the Virgin, for example Nossa Senhora de Monte, but typically a local saint may also be honoured.

The midsummer festivals were an important time for young girls, as they hoped to be given a sign about who they would marry. The junco *plant used in one of these customs, mentioned by Maria, is a type of reed, technically a type of sedge. Bulrushes are one type of sedge.*

Maria mentions that her father did not approve of the young people going to the mountains at the feast of São João. Maybe his views were the same as those of Philip Stubbes in his Anatomy of Abuses (1583). *There he says that on "May Eve folk go off, some to the woods and groves, some to the hills and mountains, here they spend the night in pastimes...I've heard it credibly reported by men of great gravity, credibility and reputation, that forty, three score, or a hundred youths, going to the woods overnight, they have scarcely the third part of them, returned home undefiled."*

At home we did not have entertainments. There was nothing like now and certainly no television – there was nothing electrical at all. But we did have a radio – it must have run on batteries – maybe my father brought it from Mozambique.

But we all looked forward to the public festivals. For us, the Easter period was very important and very special. On Shrove Tuesday we made special cakes – a sort of pancake. And you tried to eat it up that day because the next day, Ash Wednesday, was the beginning of Lent. And during that time we were not supposed to eat meat. So you couldn't eat the cake, if you had cooked it with meat fat. I'm not sure if people really didn't ever eat meat during Lent, but certainly between Ash Wednesday and Good Friday, we didn't eat meat on Fridays. And on every Friday during Lent in the evening after work we did the Stations of the Cross.

On Maundy Thursday we finished working at 1pm. We made bread that morning and at 3pm we went to the church for a ceremony.

Friday was always a special day. Our tradition says that on Fridays, we should not eat meat. But you could pay money to the church if you wanted to eat meat on Fridays – if you ate meat, you had to pay. This did not include Lent, when you were not supposed to eat meat at all, and especially not on Good Friday. I still follow this custom on that day, and I always take the day off work.

Good Friday was the biggest day of the year. Everyone respected that day – no one worked. On Good Friday you should eat less, and definitely no meat. As I said, I still follow this custom. We didn't do any work, though if you had animals, you needed to feed them. You didn't comb your hair, men didn't shave, we didn't clean the house or sweep.

We went to church wearing black, or if you didn't have anything black, you wore the darkest colours you had, like going to a funeral – because it really was Jesus' funeral.

On Good Friday there was a different ceremony from normal. The priest didn't even bless the bread. They did it the day before – normally they bless the bread in the middle of the Mass, but not on Good Friday. Then in the streets around the church there was a procession where they carried a special statue of Jesus carrying the Cross. It was called the *processão do Senhor dos Passos* (The Procession of The Lord of the Steps).

The next day, Saturday, until midday it was still the same – we didn't do much work. In the evening it was time to go to church again, and they blessed the water. And on that day a lot of people liked to baptise a child – they felt it was a good day for that.

On Easter Sunday there was a special mass. Before the mass started, two girls and three men with two flags and the cross went into the church to the altar and placed them there to open the service.

Then it was a family day and people celebrated. They killed a sheep or a goat and some people wore new clothes.

At festivals of course we had some special food. At Easter you had to have bread. And the family was coming, so you made a cake for Easter Sunday. On that day you had a nice meal.

At Easter we also had *tremoços* – they are yellow and dry. First you cook them, then because they are very sour, you have to put them in a bag in water, and soak them, so that the sourness comes out. Then you add salt, garlic and parsley with it and eat them! It is not really very nice to eat, but because we grew up with it, we want it.

Starting on Easter Sunday, there was a group of three men, two girls and a boy, often with the priest as well, who came to collect money for the church. We called it the *Visita do Divino Espirito Santo* (the Visit of the Holy Spirit). The boy carried holy water and they sprinkled it in each house. The girls sang special songs, while two of the men each carried a flag and one carried the Cross. They had a special sort of dish with a handle and a cross on it and you put your money in that. People who did not have a lot of money and so could not give much, often put the money in an envelope, so you couldn't see how much they had given.

The group did this on the following Sundays – on each Sunday they went to a different town, and they went to each house to collect money. After Easter it took about two months, almost into June. When they had finished collecting, there was a special mass again to thank everyone and to say how much money they had got.

The men belonged to the Brotherhood of the *Espirito Santo* (Holy Spirit). You had to pay to join. There was also a Brotherhood of *A Senhora Santa Ana* (the Lady, Saint Anna).

They had their own special custom. The man who carried one flag gave the group breakfast, the man with the other flag provided lunch, and the man who carried the Cross gave them dinner. The next year they changed duties, and in the third year they changed again, so they all shared the tasks.

The men wore a special top – we called it a *capa*. It was long – down to the knees, and it had no buttons or sleeves – you might call it a vest or tabard. It was made of expensive material – silk – and it was red. But if you belonged to the Brotherhood of Santa Ana it was blue, because the saint is a woman.

The girls wore a white dress and shoes, and a special hat. And they had a special sort of cape, which was red. It came over their left shoulder, but the right shoulder was not covered by it.

Next there was April 1. It's not common now to do anything special on that day, but in the old days people often played April Fool tricks. For instance, at that time there were not many phones, so someone might say "Your Mum called you" and so the person would have to walk a long distance to go to the nearest phone. Or it might just be to fool someone into looking at the floor or looking around. Then you said "*dia das petas*"(the day of lies). Or you repeated a little saying: "*uma peta fechada na gaveta*" (a lie locked in a drawer).

May 1 in my village was the Feast of the Holy Spirit. It was always a holiday and the Brotherhood came to collect money for the church. As I said, they went collecting every Sunday, but our village was special, because they always came on May 1, and that was a holiday, whatever day of the week it fell on. There were some people (you still find them) who were against religion, and they didn't want to pay, but mostly people were waiting for them to come.

On May Day you had fresh bread and cakes with the family and liqueurs – they reserve them for those special days.

But there was another custom on that day. It was about men who had done something wrong – an affair, things like that. People said those men would go somewhere to jump off a bridge, or over a bar. And they would joke with each other and say "Are you going to jump today ?"

Every town had a religious festival. In Santana it was the last Sunday of July – the feast of Santa Ana and the first Sunday of August was São Joaquim's day.

In July we also celebrated three special saints' days – Santo Antonio (St Antony) was June 13, São João (St John) was June 24 and São Pedro (St Peter) is June 29. On São João and Santo Antonio we decorated outside our front door with an arch of flowers.

On the festival days there were stalls around the church. They sold milk and we bought some meat, which we boiled. And the next day in the evening we made soup again, but we added pasta. You bought one packet – it was not a kilo – you could buy different amounts. One kilo of pasta would last for several meals in that stew.

You celebrate São Pedro by the sea. We went from our village to the coast, but our sea is very rough, so we walked over the pebble beach and rocks just to paddle, though my father didn't approve!

The feast of San João was for the sheep, so it was a festival in the mountains, because that is where the sheep were. We would go almost to the mountains, because there was a house there, like a tourist house, and some people came from the city to stay there. And there was another beautiful house for the wardens who looked after the forest. We walked there. I remember being with this group when my father was in Jersey – because if he had been at home, he wouldn't have let us go!

Santo Antonio was the patron saint of engagements. In Santana there is a small chapel dedicated to him and the young people prayed there to the saint to help them get married – that day they hoped to find a boyfriend – but I never did that. Some girls used to beat their breasts hard when they prayed, and people would tease them and say they needed to take a rock to do it!

In the evening before the festival, when it was getting dark, the church bell rang, and we made a fire and jumped over it. To get the atmosphere, you jump over the fire. And we had carnations. You threw the flowers into the fire, and then waited for someone to come. If someone – a man – passed at that time, we said he (or someone of the same name, if he was married) was going to marry the last girl who threw a carnation before he arrived – we made those kinds of joke. Some girls used to throw the carnation when no one was looking, because they didn't want to be teased. It was nice.

There was another custom, which I never took part in, but some of my neighbours did. They went to a banana tree with a knife and stuck it in the tree. When you do that a liquid comes out, a bit like resin from a pine tree. They looked to see if the liquid spelled out a name on that tree – that would be the man you would marry. But sometimes nothing happened straightaway, so they left the knife in the tree and the next day they went to see if a name had appeared. But the owners of the trees didn't like it, because they said it killed the tree.

There was another custom with *junco* – it's a sort of grass – I did do this one. It grows on wet land and the animals didn't like it, so we didn't use it for them. We put it together, and tied it up, and you cut the stalks at the same point. Then you wrote names on bits of paper and tied those round the stalks. The next day you go there to check what has happened. Some of the grass didn't grow but some did and so was longer than the others. The name on the longest one was the man you were going to marry. But you didn't tell anybody, because you didn't want to be teased.

Another thing was that you filled a big glass with water and then you broke an egg into the glass. Sometimes nothing happened – nothing showed. If you were not lucky, nothing grew. But if you were, you could read your future, because the egg grows inside the glass. You see things come up. So people might imagine an aeroplane, and that meant they would go on a journey. Sometimes it showed a lot of things. The more it showed, the more lucky you were. But some parents didn't like it, because they thought it was wasting an egg! That custom was very important for the village, because it was about boyfriends and girlfriends, and you were curious.

Sweets were always special then. We had them especially in the July festivals. When I was a teenager I had a few *tostões* (name of old coin worth 10 *centavos*) – someone had given them to me and I saved them. For one *tostão* you could get two sweets and I had about five *tostões*. During the festival you got different sweets on the stalls from what you got in the shops. I brought the sweets home to eat when I felt like it – it was the first time I had my own sweets.

There was also the Festival of the Seven Saints – they were all women. This took place on August 15th. It was a holiday and we had to go to church. That day there was more than one priest to celebrate the mass, and they sang different music. People liked to go to ask for forgiveness or help.

There were seven saints in seven different places. So we had an open truck and people from the village used to go to them on that. For the whole way they sang. And they took some food with them – boiled potatoes, bread, fruit. When we got to the new place, we went to the church – because it was a saint's day, you had to go to church. People wore their best clothes, because at that time there weren't many places to visit. Then the church was more important. Now it isn't, because people have more things to do for entertainment.

At the church there was a mass, and then there was a procession and the image of the saint for that town was carried around the church. Sometimes it was a big procession and sometimes short. And the people put flowers on the streets – everyone had flowers in their garden and on their land – in fact there is a saying "*Madeira é um jardim*" (Madeira is a garden). Then they stayed in the street to watch the procession. Some were wearing special traditional clothes.

Before the festival, some people went to the mountains to get *louro* (bay) tree branches. Then the day before the festival started, they made a stall with a wood frame, and covered it with the branches and leaves. They killed cows, and hung them from the roof of the stall, and cut off slices as required. They made a fire and cooked the beef, with salt and garlic, on a bay skewer (we call it *espatada)*. Now they use metal because it is easier, but the meat tasted better on the bay skewers. Nowadays it's not that common to do this, because there are the laws about hygiene, and the animals have to go to a slaughterhouse to be killed. But then you could kill your animal at home, or even at the festival. Now it has to be a proper butcher, like here.

I mentioned the people who collected money for the church. In November they came to the village with the statue of Santa Ana to collect money again. There was special custom that, if a person died who had contributed, the people who collected money went to the funeral wearing their red top. It was compulsory, a kind of respect. My father never contributed, so when he was buried, people didn't wear their tops.

The festival of São Martinho (St Martin) was on November 11. It was the first day of the new wine. You went to friends to taste the wine and have *castanhas (*chestnuts) – they always had chestnuts – and perhaps some *bacalhau* – certainly something to eat.

A very special treat was *pão por deu* – a special sort of bread. My mother made the bread with corn flour – it was round bread – you make it with a different dough. It's not the same as wheat flour – the corn flour is much heavier. And my mum put in some herbs. One is star anis and to make it sweeter a bit of sugar and some salt. You can't eat the star anis seeds. Instead you boil them and use the liquid in making the bread. You have it just once a year. We loved that bread because it was sweet and different. But at that time my mum also made dough balls with the brown (wheat germ) flour. On the first day we had to eat those and the next day we had the *pão por deus*.

During the festival some people would go around to the houses to sing, sometimes with instruments. They still do it.

Boas Festas!

The title is the Portuguese way of wishing you "Merry Christmas and Happy New Year." In modern Britain, preparations may begin months early and the festivities may now take place over something like six weeks. But in Maria's youth, in Santana, these were luxuries not to be thought of. Instead just the main church festivals were free days, greatly looked forward to, because they provided rest and treats with the family, at a time of year when there was less work than usual.

Some of these days will be unfamiliar to many British people. The first, on 8 December, is the Feast of the Immaculate Conception. It celebrates the day on which the Virgin Mary was conceived, according to Catholic belief, without the stain of Original Sin.

Maria speaks affectionately of the missas do parto, *held for nine days before Christmas. The masses celebrate the* Expectação do Parto da Beatíssima Virgem Maria *(awaiting the giving of birth by the Blessed Virgin Mary –* parto *means "parturition", giving birth).*

⟨⟩

In the autumn we started to feed the animals to fatten them for Christmas. The pigs we slaughtered in December. From 1 December at the weekends everyone got their family and friends together to slaughter the pigs. At those weekends you saw so many fires, because they singed the skin of the pig to remove the hairs. Some time before, people went and cut and dried two special sorts of wood, *urze* (heather) and *feiteira* (fern) ready for that time. In December they made fires with those plants and everywhere there was the smell of them. People would stop to look and said "Ah, our neighbour killed his pig today" or "They are going to kill their pig next week."

After the pig was killed, there was still a lot to do. First, when you singed the pig. It made the skin black, so they had to clean it with a scraper. It needed a lot of water, so you had to keep fetching water from the spring. That was hard work!

Next they hung the pig up and split it down the middle, so they could remove the intestines. Then the women took the intestines to the stream to clean them. That took a long time, You had a group of women and they had first to separate the intestines and scrape off any fat with a knife. Then they turned them inside out, like you do with a sock, so they could scrape the inside. That was very important, because that is where all the pig dung was. It had to be adults and people who were careful, so that the job was done properly.

Once the intestines were clean, they were boiled – you needed to do that on the same day. You added lemon and orange to take the smell away. You could cook them after they were cold if you wanted, but usually we added salt and lemon skins – that was to make less smell. Then after a few days they could cook them. But you had to boil them again, because there was a lot of salt.

Sometimes they left some pigs until the beginning of January to be slaughtered, because there was not enough time to deal with them all – it all took a long time, a whole day – that's why they did it at the weekends, when they had more time. It was also a sort of family celebration.

Another thing was that, with a female pig, they sometimes waited till January, because the pig was in season. That's the special time when the female wants the male pig. Sometimes they would go to prepare the animal, but they could see that she was in season and so they didn't kill it, because they said the meat was not good.

For the religious side of the festival, we began on 8 December – it is the Feast of the Immaculate Conception. On that day we put wheat seeds in water, to plant one week before Christmas around the *presepio* – the manger where the Baby Jesus lies.

Then for nine days before Christmas, very early in the morning – at 5am or 6 am – they have a special mass – it's called *missa do parto* and they sing Christmas songs. I like to go to that ceremony because it is the beginning of Christmas. People used to go off to work afterwards, but now they organise a little party. They have a drink and a sandwich outside the church. And people bring things such as chicken soup and drink coffee, or a liqueur or *aguardente* or brandy and biscuits. And they sing outside the church. Then about 7.30 or 8 they go to work, and they feel happy. After we left the mass, we sang on the way home and people never complained. But now people complain about noise and about the church bells.

On Christmas Eve or the day before almost everyone prepared the Christmas feast. They baked bread, cake and biscuits – we didn't buy much, we made it. On Christmas Eve everyone was busy, everyone contributed for Christmas Day. During the day we killed chickens – we are not allowed to kill chickens on Christmas Day – and cleaned the house like a full spring clean.

When you kill the chickens, there are things you have to do. First you hang them with the head at the bottom. This is to let the blood drain out – if you don't do that the flesh is very dark. Then you boil water, and when it is hot, you dip the chicken in it. That makes it easier to pull out the feathers. If you could, you did this with the right moon – people said that when the moon was at a certain point, small feathers grew, which were harder to pull out. People did a lot of things according to the moon then.

There was a lot of baking. At Christmas we first made bread and when the bread was cooked and the oven was heated, it was enough to cook a cake – about a kilo in weight. My mum used to make *bolo preto* – it was a family cake. You need to separate the eggs – it needs a lot of eggs for that cake. You have eggs, milk, flour, the skin of an orange or lemon and bit of wine. *Bolo preto* was easier and cheaper than the yellow one, the *bolo de família*. Every Christmas a lot of people have *bolo de mela* (honey cake), but we never made it in our mother's house, because it is expensive to make. So it was very very special, but now it's much more common. It was not made with bees' honey, you use *mela de cana* (sugar cane honey). You need to put in dry ingredients, then soak it in wine for a while, before you cook it. When it is cooked, it looks smaller.

We would also have the famous Madeira cake, but we had it at other times as well. My *bolo* (Madeira cake) is light because of the ingredients. You take wheat flour and squeeze in the juice of an orange, and some sugar, but not too much. You need to beat the white of eggs and after you put that together with the yolks, and it becomes more soft.

Often we had the *bolo* with a liqueur – you made the liqueur yourself. You bought alcohol from the pharmacy, then you added water to make it the strength or weakness you wanted. You boiled the water and added the flavouring, which also came from the pharmacy. It was a very fine powder. There were a lot of different tastes: *morango* (strawberry), vanilla, banana, tangerine. You let it cool then mixed it with the alcohol. The longer you leave the liqueur, the more smooth it tastes.

You could also add things to *aguardente,* like sugar cane, or if you had a beehive, bees' honey. But then honey was mostly used as a medicine and was very expensive, so we didn't use much. But now they add a lot, or they add natural fruits, such as passion fruit, and some water. Then they leave it to boil again.

We had other treats, too. And on Christmas Eve we set up the Christmas tree. We went to the woods to find a nice tree. In the mountains there is a different tree, like the ones you get here. But you couldn't get that unless you went a long way. So we went to our woods and found a nice tree and decorated it with balloons, and if we had any Christmas cards, we put them round the tree. We used leaves of *azevinho* (holly) and *largacampo* (a local evergreen) to decorate the house, especially in the sitting room.

On the evening of Christmas Eve we didn't go to bed at the usual time – we carried on preparing, we ate at 9 o'clock, and got ready to go to the church at midnight.

When you got to the church, it had the lights off and the Angel started to sing – they still it do it – and when the Angel sings, they ring the bells very hard, and the lights come on and the other angels around the altar sing as a choir. They are really children wearing clothes like an angel and they sing special songs. Near the altar they decorate the *presepio* – the Nativity scene with the Baby Jesus. And they have a big Christmas tree.

For a week before this mass, people from our area and from the different villages around made groups and prepared to sing in a procession for the Baby Jesus. They did this after the Mass. We waited until that was finished, because we enjoyed it. I remember that when we left the church, it was nearly daylight, because there were 23 groups to sing. They came from the church door towards the altar. They sang, they stopped, then they moved on a bit. They sang for the priest and the Baby Jesus, and they said they had come from far away to see the Christ child. You feel a lot of emotions and you feel happy, because you have celebrated it.

When we went home, maybe at four in the morning, you saw your friends or family, who knew you were going to pass by. You dropped in for a liqueur and cake – it was made the day before, but you didn't eat it till then – you weren't allowed, because it was for Christmas!

Afterwards there were presents, but not always in the old days, because there was no money. When you got presents, you were not allowed to open them before midnight. So you opened them when you came home after the church. I remember when my son was small, he wanted to open his presents and I said "No, you have to go to the church first, and afterwards you can open them." So he was always keen to go to the church on that day, so he could open his presents!

Now it's Father Christmas who is said to give the presents, but then it was always Baby Jesus. Later they gave surprises to the children, but then they gave what the children needed

– there were not many toys. But in our case we were lucky. We had some toys, because my auntie came from the city. As I said, we opened them on Christmas Day after we came from the church. We put shoes around the fire to put the presents in. But I remember that one time my father played a trick on my sisters – he put a sickle for cutting grass on top of the shoes. My sister was furious! Another time he would move the shoes out of the room. So sometimes my sisters waited for my father, to be sure that he didn't come to the kitchen and take the shoes away!

Then you went to bed to sleep a bit.

In the morning we carried on again, to enjoy the drink, the food, talking, wearing our nice clothes – on Christmas Day you didn't work. Yes, you had to see to the animals – that happened every day – but apart from that, nothing. It was a very special day, and it still is very special for us.

On Christmas Day in the morning you maybe got up at 9am. We had meat (pork) – we call it *carne de vinhadalhos* – we had to have that! We prepared it a few days before and marinaded it. You cut the pork into small pieces and you fry it. We cooked it with pinewood. When you marinade it, there is a sauce. We keep the sauce and when the meat is fried, you add more sauce and more wine and you put a slice of bread on top of the meat, and cover it with a lid so that it gets the steam and the tastes. For breakfast we had that and coffee – or wine – because the meat is salty, you feel like drinking wine.

After that we went to my grandmother's house. My mum wanted us all to be at her house, but my grandmother never accepted. You get married, but on Christmas Day all the family have to come together, and she had the space and so we all could all sit down round the table.

At lunch time, we had a different kind of meal – chicken – chicken soup or stew – with a lot of things together, or a meat stew with rice and potatoes.

Then at night time we had to have rice. I remember my grandmother always had rice and chicken at night time, before you left their house.

There was no transport, and it was a long way, but we walked all the way there and back. When we came back, it was dark of course, unless there was a moon that night. But we knew the way so well we could do it without looking down – we could even cross streams on stepping stones.

Boxing Day, as long as I remember, was always at my mum's house, and just for us and my auntie from the city. She always came to spend Christmas with us. On Boxing Day we had a different meal – we didn't cook the same as we did on Christmas Day. Sometimes we had pork, cabbage, sweet potatoes, potatoes and yams all together, and a lot of meat for lunch. In the evening we had chicken cooked in a different way from the day before.

But on Boxing Day we liked to have tripe. We cleaned it, washed and boiled it, then threw the water away and salted it. If the animal was old, it took longer to cook. You let it cool then you fry onions, a lot of onions, garlic, lemon or orange – my grandmother had an orange tree and you could get fruit at Christmas. We saved some to put round the Baby Jesus. Then you take puréed tomato and rosemary and fry it together. You add the tripe and let it cook on a low fire for a long time. When it is cooked you add anything else you want – potatoes – small potatoes – *pipinellos* (gherkins) and sweet potatoes. After you can put some pasta with it or eat it with boiled potatoes or rice.

Or we cooked pumpkins. You cook them in the same way. But you don't add water, because if you do, the pumpkins separate – they need to be together like a purée. So it takes longer to cook because they need to be melted. If you want, you can cook it together with the tripe and when it's nearly cooked, you add potatoes. We loved it and we still cook it, if not on Boxing Day, some time round Christmas.

After that you ate lots of cakes and biscuits, fresh and home-made – it's not like now, it was good and nobody complained!

After Christmas the first weekend was another special day – we call it the *Dia da Sagrada Familha* (Feast of the Holy Family).

Then on New Year's Eve we went to my auntie's – it was like Christmas, with the family being together. They had a special celebration – there were fireworks all over the city, even in the port. You went out to a place where you could see it.

6 January (Epiphany) was another special day. We had a special cake called *bolo do rei*. When we were young, my auntie brought one from the city, because we didn't have it. There was a mass at midday, and then some people made a group and went to the houses to sing. If they came to your house, they sang, and you could go with them if you wanted. Some people had instruments, things like a guitar and violin and a triangle.

We kept the Christmas tree decorations even after the 6th. Then at the end of January there was the feast of São Sebastião and they said that day was the day to clean all the cupboards to see if you had anything left over!

Love and Marriage

Maria shows that when young people got married, as now, it was a big event. But then there was little money, so that things we take for granted now, such as eating chicken, were very special.

It was a society where a girl was supposed to remain a virgin until she married. But, as has always happened, this ideal was not always followed. Then, if she could not keep her condition secret, there was usually shame and social rejection.

⟜

If you wanted to get married, and if your parents accepted it, the girl's parents went to the boy's parents to talk about marriage. But before the boy asked the girl to marry him, he had to ask her father for permission. After you had met both lots of parents, you didn't wait much then. In my time there were no engagement rings, just wedding rings. These were provided by godparents.

In Portugal, there are three sets of godparents – the *padrinho de batismo* (for baptism), the *padrinho de confirmação* (for Confirmation) and the *padrinho de casamento* (for weddings). They can be the same people, or different. For a wedding the parents and the bride and groom looked for two couples to sign the register and be godparents. One of the couples needed to give a big present for the wedding – the wedding rings and a big dish. But you had to have the money to pay for it. Some people had been godparents of many people. If you asked a couple, and they couldn't afford it, that was all right – you asked someone else. The second pair of godparents gave a present, but less expensive than the first couple.

But it could be quite complicated! Many people didn't want to go to someone and be refused. If the couple said no, nobody went there again. They didn't want to be rejected. And some people who were asked were unhappy about being chosen as the second pair of godparents. In poor families, you often chose a family member – I chose my auntie – because really we couldn't afford to keep giving presents.

You were supposed not to have sex before the marriage, but of course, some girls did. And some of them found they were pregnant. If you got pregnant, you needed to get married. So they tried to get married straight away and cover it. Sometimes they got married very late in the pregnancy, but it was very rare to have a child before you got married.

Normally if you were a boy and you got a girl pregnant, you had to marry her. If you didn't marry her, it was bad news for the girl. Even if your boyfriend left you, it meant a bad name for the girl, and often no one wanted her, because she had already had a boyfriend. And people gossiped and said "She is not a virgin." Some girls got married afterwards, but there were ones who never did, because nobody wanted them. Then they stayed at home and worked. It was not because she was not a good person, but nobody respected her.

If a girl got pregnant, and the boy did not want to marry her, people didn't always know. Now girls often wear clothes that are very tight, but at that time you didn't have that fashion, so not many people saw the signs of pregnancy. Then when the baby was born, often she just stayed with her family, and worked around the house, and on the land, and the baby grew up in the family with the aunties. But what they did was, they treated that child like a sister or brother, and so the child called the aunties its sisters.

There was a lady in our area – she had three girls – the oldest was my age. That lady lived on her own. I don't know anything about her husband, but she had a bad reputation, as she had sex with so many men. Men went there for the night and had sex with her. So she had a bad name, like a prostitute. People didn't want to talk to her, but I was married and I was already working with her, and so I did talk to her. But she never told us about the bad things she did – she did them, but she didn't try to get anyone else to do the same.

In the city there were brothels, but not in the village. But in Santana we had another lady who had a bad reputation. Maybe she had had a child with another man or maybe she didn't, but she did have sex with other men. The men were proud and boasted "I've been with her." But you just had one woman like that in different places, as if here there was one in Highgate and one in Victoria.

Women like that had a bad name, but they were not always a bad person. We had one I remember well. She had had a child by another man and if something happened like that everyone knew, but everyone loved her. She was very poor and very old and she used to beg for food. She came from down the end of Santana. She walked everywhere and she asked nicely for a bite to eat and for *esmola* (alms). Of course, not many people gave her money, because few of us had money to give away. But food they would give, things like *trigo* (wheat), *milho* (maize), potatoes – anything like that that lasted – even salted pork. She had a daughter, who at that time was young, and sometimes she brought the girl with her. Then someone came at the end of the day to carry the bag with whatever she collected to feed the family.

But you could also have a poor family that behaved badly and had a lot of children. The children were very badly brought up, and went out on their own, begging for food. People didn't respect those children or the family. That poor lady, though, nobody refused to give her something.

Once an engagement was announced, people went to the shops around, and chose presents. They got *linho* and tea towels and *trigo, milho* and potatoes, because the couple were starting a new family and a new life. So people bought plates, cutlery – anything for the kitchen. They felt that the couple needed all things they had at home – even live chickens!

The weddings happened on a Saturday. But on the Saturday before, at night, they invited the young girls who were the bride's friends to make the bed for the new couple. When they made it, they played tricks, like putting needles in the bed, and painting pictures of men's and women's parts. One would put on the sheet, and another did something funny – and sometimes they even tore the bedsheet. But it was a happy time.

The young men were around the house outside and some people wanted to look through the window, so the friends covered the windows. Then people would try tricks to get them to open the bedroom door. At last they opened the door and showed all that they had done, but only to other girls – not the boys – and not the bride or groom.

Meanwhile some people cooked and made special bread – you had to have biscuits, and a lot of the bread – we call it *bolo de noiva* (fiancée's cake) – it was a busy night.

On the Sunday they went to church early in the morning and then went back home. There were people in the house, waiting to invite the neighbours. The Sunday before the wedding was the day for receiving the presents. The bride had to be at home for people to come with their presents, which they put on the bed. Sometimes they were wrapped, if they were bought in a shop. But often they weren't, so you didn't have a lot of unwrapping of presents.

The people stayed there for a while, and they had wine and different kinds of liqueur, which they put on a tray – the bride's family had to serve liqueurs, biscuits, bread and butter – it had to be butter at that time. Also, if you brought a present, they gave you *bolo de noiva*. It was only made for weddings. Everyone wanted it, because it was sweet and different. The first day it is very sweet and soft, but the next day it gets harder.

During the week the couple carried on working – their normal life. Then the day before the wedding they had to make bread and kill chickens for the wedding day. But the presents were still on the bed.

At the church you wore a white dress if you were not pregnant, and you gave a bunch of flowers to the statue of Mary, because you were a virgin. If they were pregnant and could hide it, they wore white, like they were a virgin, and they still gave the flowers. But if you got married when you were pregnant, at say six months, when the baby showed, you got married but in a different church – somewhere far away and with a simple ceremony, and not in white.

People put on good clothes for the wedding. Just the aunties, uncles, grandparents and brothers went to the church, but the bride's mum and sisters didn't go – they stayed at home and cooked and so on. Now you have bridesmaids, but then they didn't. But you did have a young boy and a young girl who had recently taken their first Communion, because they could wear their Communion white clothes. And of course there were the godparents.

The day before the wedding they prepared a big basket for the godparents – they put in chicken and cakes – the sort of things you were going to have on the day. Then the bride took it to them.

On the wedding day, when they went to the church, there was no transport, so they had to walk from the house to the church and then walk back. When the road was made, they went by car. But before, when you came from the church, people from the area waited on the street, because they knew when the married couple would come back. And they went in front of them to throw flowers – at the time it was roses. And the people went up to them with a basket with biscuits, even a liqueur. Now they don't do it, because they have huge cars.

When the wedding group got home, they had a meal. At a wedding they try to cook more than the main dishes. They had a special cook, someone who cooked well, and they invited her to come to cook for them. Before the day they invited that lady to come to the house, and talked to her and decided how much rice, butter and fish and so on they needed. Then during the week they had to go to the city (Funchal) in a taxi to buy the things for the day.

One of the things they collected was the wedding cake, which was made in Funchal. But it was not easy to bring it back! At that time the roads were very bad, so the car could jerk a lot, and if you were not careful, the cake could get broken or smashed. So two people sat in the back seat to hold it and protect it.

The wedding feast filled the whole house. As I explained before, the most important room in the house was the sitting room. They pulled out the table and put the chairs round it. But the room was very small, so around the table it just had to be the special people – just the uncles and parents and grandparents – not even the sisters or brothers – there was no space, because the room was so small. And those special people had plates and glasses. Most people were too poor to have their own sets of crockery, so they borrowed them from richer neighbours.

The rest of the family and the guests were in the kitchen, or just outside, if it was warm weather. If they were going to be outside, they made a special place – we called it a *barraca*. It was a sort of big shed, where the guests could get together. Nowadays people would have a marquee. But this was made specially from bay tree branches with a roof and walls of bay leaves. Afterwards they put the branches and leaves on the land. The leaves rotted and went into the earth, and the branches were used for firewood – as I have often said, nothing was wasted!

And there was an important difference from modern parties. For these guests, there was just one glass. Someone filled it, handed it to you, you drank it straight away in one or two goes, and handed it back. Then they did the same for the next person.

Before my time, it was even more different. Poorer people didn't have glasses. Instead they drank out of a cow's horn. They were good, because they didn't break easily, unlike glass. I remember my father had one, but really it was more of a souvenir. But for the people before him it was normal.

They invited the priest to come to the meal and before they ate, he blessed the food, and them, and prayed. If the priest couldn't come in time, they prayed anyway.

They carried on late into the night. Now they have singing and dancing, but before they all sat around the table and they talked and ate. When they had finished, they came out of the room, and talked to each other, and to the bride as well.

Later, in the evening, they went and ate another meal, and when that was finished, they stood up and prayed around the table.

When the guests left, the couple needed to take the things from off the bed before they could sleep. But they knew what their friends had done, when they found a lot of difficulties, especially the needles! So by the time they got to bed, sometimes it was very late. For instance, they might find the bed sheet was torn – the friends had ripped the sheets. So they needed new sheets and they were impatient and they didn't like it! And another thing was that people were listening outside. When they left the house, it was very dark – there were no lights or electricity – so they could come back without being seen. They wanted to know what went on in the night, and they hid around the house to hear the noises.

Sometimes they played more tricks. I remember when my cousin was married, someone put a tape recorder under the bed. He was a man who always talked a lot, even on his wedding night! So afterwards they teased him a lot!

On the next day they wanted to know if the bedsheets were messy – some people were curious and they wanted to see. And the next day when they tidied up, if they didn't see the sheet was dirty, they talked!

On the Sunday they carried on with the celebration, but they also tidied up and washed the dishes, especially the ones they had borrowed from people for the guests at the table. That day they ate, drank and tidied up.

A Courtship

Maria married early. Because of the very traditional nature of the society she lived in, she was able to do so at the age of 17, which was clearly against Portuguese law, but not necessarily against custom.

Maria makes clear that she drifted into marriage, and that she now finds it hard to decide why. But she makes it clear how little opportunity women had to be independent and shape their own lives. Really, her attitude at the time – now happily greatly changed! – was a dull acceptance of how things had to be. This viewpoint was so deeply ingrained that she – and presumably many women like her – did not even imagine that things could be different.

She also shows the very real belief in magic, always carried out in the village by women. Among the practices she describes is the carrying of a small bag containing objects thought to be protective against harm. This is a practice found all over the world – the object has various names, for example "phylactery", the bag worn by observant Jews and containing texts from the Torah, as a reminder of the goodness of God.

A lot of girls in their teens spend most of their time thinking about boys. But I was not interested in getting involved with boys – I don't know why. The boys would go to wait outside the church and see the girls pass by to go home, and they would talk to them. Sometimes one would follow you. There were a few that were interested in me – I think there were four at that time who wanted to follow me. But I didn't give them a chance, because I walked with my mum or with friends. I didn't ever think of getting married.

But when I was 16, there was a boy called Antonio. He was local and he liked me. He worked in a sort of corner shop very close to our house, and I went there often to get things. He was good looking, but I didn't fancy him!

He came to work with us, because my father was not at home. He was three years older than me. He started to follow me. It was easy for him, because when you work together on a farm, it's like being friends. And I joked and talked with everyone. But his mind was more in advance than mine! He fancied me. People began to say things to us like "She likes you" and "He likes you" – things like that. When people say things like that, sometimes things get closer. People knew he came to our house to work for us and they said "He's Maria's boyfriend."

But he never left me alone and he didn't give the other boys a chance to come round me. He waited to follow me to the church and when I finished church, he followed me home. When I went to work on the land, he would go to meet me as I came by. Antonio never left me a gap to go anywhere on my own, or let people come up and talk to me.

At that time there was a boy I knew from Santana who liked me, and used to follow me from the church. The boy was one of our neighbours, and I was friends with his sisters. But Antonio found out that the boy liked me, so he stopped him – he argued with him in the shop.

There was one boy – he was a nice guy – and his auntie invited me to go to work for them. Really she wanted me to meet this guy, her nephew. I still wasn't interested in marriage and I didn't give him an opportunity to be close with me. I knew what they wanted – it was not an arranged marriage, they just wanted to give the opportunity for us to get together. But Antonio closed all the gates.

When we got closer, people began to talk and spread gossip, but I just followed him, like a chicken follows the cock. My mum was very angry and she said to his mum that he had debts, and his mum denied it. After I got married, I found that he did have debts.

He carried on working for us and I talked to him nicely. But people also said bad things about him, that he was bad, that he destroyed things at home, that he shouted at his Mum. But we didn't know the truth at the time, because his mother covered up for him.

I remember many times when I was in the countryside, I tried to avoid going the way where he would meet me. But I didn't have the courage and the strength to make the decision. I believe it was because I was too young. Even the day before I got married, I hid in someone's house because Antonio was aggressive to me. Because she knew him, my cousin said to me "Maria, it would be better to have a baby in your arms, than to marry him." But I never made a decision; what he said, I followed.

Then he said he wanted to marry me. But my father was in Jersey, so Antonio asked me to write a letter to send to my father. I wrote it and gave it to Antonio. I don't remember what I wrote. I don't know exactly what happened then. He made the decisions and I just followed. I was young and I didn't have any other way to go. So my father left Jersey earlier that year and came back to Madeira. My auntie wrote from Jersey and said my father was not happy about it, because I was very young. My mum was worried, because she didn't agree with the marriage. In fact, not a single person in my family thought it was a good idea.

As I said, when I started to go with him, I was 16, and I was married at 17. But I don't know how that happened. In Portugal you were supposed to be 18 to get married.

I know that he decided to go to the church and talk to the priest. I never said "I don't want to" – I just shrugged my shoulders. Naturally we had a priest; he had been in that area for many years and they said he used to arrange marriages. So my mum and I and Antonio went to the church for a meeting and on the way my mum was very huffy, because she didn't agree with it, but she went anyway. And she said to the priest, "She is going to get married, but I don't approve of it."

I don't know what the priest did. He must have written a letter or filled in a form. My mum needed to sign but she didn't sign, because she cannot write. Then Antonio went to the Registry Office to take the papers. At that time they closed at midday for lunch and so he waited till two o' clock with the papers. But I never went to the Registry Office to get married. Maybe the priest said something, I don't know. They just wanted people to get married – if you didn't it was bad thing.

After that, the priest asked Antonio where he wanted to get married. By this time my father had changed his attitude, so because my parents didn't agree between themselves, Antonio decided to go the city (Funchal) and get married in a church, called São Pedro – it was the one where my mother was married. Again I didn't disagree and just followed.

The day when we went to the church, there was my father, Antonio's mum, and my grandfather, my brother Manuel, two children and two aunts who lived in Funchal. There was just a small car as there were only six of us. We went, we got married and came back. I didn't have the strength to say no.

I don't know where my brains were. We carried on for years – it seemed I had to. But it wasn't true that you don't have the right to disagree. I wasn't in love with him then – nor ever in my life. I like him for some things, but not love. Love to me has to be love, true love, not just about liking someone. I still don't believe in love.

After getting married, I worked on the land again, but on a farm of our own. At that time I didn't have any big cows, just small ones. That was because big cows need a lot of good grass for them to give milk. But small ones will eat anything. We killed them when they were one year old. That was better for us, because we didn't have our own bit of land – we rented. My wish was to have land to which belonged to me and Antonio – he had never owned land, he always rented. I say "rent" but that time when you rented land, you didn't pay money. Instead what you earned from the produce was divided: three parts for the owner and one for the worker. Some people are rich in land and then it costs them nothing – they just take their share.

I mentioned that my father had changed his view. I am still not sure why this was – after all, he came back early from Jersey, because he was anxious about the marriage. But some people said that black magic had been used on my father.

Certainly, at first my father was very, very angry when he found out that I was seeing Antonio. My family thought he was coming back to Madeira to beat me or even kill me – they were very worried about it.

But when my father came home, Antonio met him. I don't know what he said, but my father never ever again said a word against him or even against me. Antonio was very jealous and aggressive towards me and swore at me. Yet my father was never against him and always talked to him nicely. So people said there was something wrong there – the way my father was before and then how he was after he met Antonio – it looked like black magic was working – but I don't know if it's true or not.

Certainly there were people who said they could do black magic, but it was particular people – not everyone did it. One thing they did was to read cards. Another was that some people went to the cemetery and brought certain branches to give to the lady to make black magic – it was always a lady. Sometimes they took their used clothes, even underwear. And when something was missing, they turned to black magic. They made black magic to make people get married and or to get separated. In fact, they still do it and they get money for it.

One method they did was to spread a kind of powder in the area where someone lived. I can give an example – it's about my aunt – everyone was scared of her. She called people names and destroyed their families' reputations.

Anyway I was separated from Antonio, when my first son, David, was four years old, because Antonio had been very aggressive to me. I stayed in my Mum's house for three months with David. One day my auntie came there – that was unusual for her to come to see me. I was in my bedroom – it was night time.

My aunt talked to me. Then when I left the house, the floor was white – she had spread powder all over. People said she did that to make me go back to Antonio. Certainly, after it happened, I went back to him.

Another thing was the "evil eye." You can wear a cross or something blessed by the Church, in a medallion. It might be special herbs, or leaves like on Palm Sunday. Or they keep them in a small bag – people wore it inside their bras or somewhere like that. Antonio gave me something like that before I got married, to protect me from other people doing me harm.

Like I said, the people who did black magic often made people afraid of them. But I remember one man who made what I think was "white magic." After David was born, he had some health problems and he had asthma. So we went to a man in the city. They said he was very clever, and understood how to be healthy. He made a sort of tea with some herbs and so on, and it helped. I think the reason why he treated people was not really for money, it was for his own spirit. Sometimes he was able to help people, who hadn't seemed to have a cure. So there were always a lot of people waiting to see him.

Pregnancy and Childbirth

Maria gives further insight into the hard lives of women when she describes childbirth. Many babies died, and there was no real support for the bereaved mother. And there was hostility towards women finding out about contraception. In view of current debates about sexual matters in the Catholic Church, Maria gives us another perspective. There was no doubt about the religious faith of the people. But being poor and lacking control of their lives in many ways, they found whatever practical ways they could to deal with the harsh realities.

The picture Maria gives of becoming a mother is very different from what is expected in modern Britain. The very survival of the baby – or the mother – could not be taken for granted, and knowledge about pregnancy and infancy depended on the willingness of other women to tell you. And this was not certain – it is clear that these were matters which you didn't talk about. Until Maria was an adult there was no clinic and little professional medical support. But at the same time the child became linked to the family and godparents by very close bonds, which Maria has already described at times.

After you were married, when you got pregnant, you kept it secret. You didn't talk much about it. You carried on working and there wasn't discussion about the pregnancy like now. Some people, like old ladies and so on, gave you advice, but not that much. It was not very open.

When you were pregnant, they said you should eat chicken. If you didn't have any, neighbours would bring a half chicken or whatever. There was not much meat, but it just makes a nice taste. And it's good for the stomach.

When women had a baby, it was born at home. In later years you went to the hospital, but earlier you had the baby at your home and if you died, you died; if you didn't die, you survived.

The hospital was far away and there was no transport. Later you went by bus or in a car or taxi and often you had the baby in the taxi. It happened so many times because the hospital was far away.

When our mother had a baby, we were curious, but they didn't want children around – they sent you to a neighbour's or something.

We had two or three ladies in Santana who delivered the babies. Then they would come every day for a week to wash the baby and to advise people what to do – how to put a nappy on and so on. This happened with me, when I had my first child, David.

After the baby was born, they gave the mother light food that was good for the milk. They give milk to the mother or some soups. They often made chicken soup and in the old days they bought a little pasta from the shop to go with it. I remember when my younger sister was born, my father made chicken soup for my mum. But we weren't allowed to eat any of it!

When they were breast feeding, the mothers didn't eat everything that they usually did. I remember that onion is not good and the child gets pus in its eye. If the mother eats something that is not good, the child suffers.

At that time, when you had a baby, they gave presents to the mother – like a packet of sugar or maybe half a chicken, a half kilo of pasta or a bar of soap. It wasn't very often clothes for the baby, because they didn't have many clothes. But when they baptised the child in our area, the godmother gave the baby a dress for the christening.

Another christening tradition was for the *padrinhos de batismo* – the christening godparents – to give a gift, usually a necklace. If they could afford it, they would give one made of gold. But people understood that many people were very poor, so it was fine to give a silver necklace, or even no present at all. This happened for both boys and girls, and many people continued to wear them when they grew up, and not just on special occasions. My son David has continued this custom.

For the christening, the mother didn't go to the church, because they were not well. At that time they stayed in bed for longer and the baby was baptised very soon after. And when the people came from the church after a christening, there was a party rather like a wedding. I still remember the party for my sister, the youngest, that we had in our sitting room.

But after that, it was not the end of the matter. At Christmas, Boxing Day or New Year, you took a basket and presents to the godparents, like happened at a wedding. And they took a live chicken. If the child was very small, the parents carried it. But when the child could walk, and was old enough, they went to the godparents' house by themselves with a live chicken and produce that the family had grown. Sometimes the godparents made a meal, because they knew the child would come with a chicken, and had a party.

They always chose a good chicken for the godparents. Even here in London some people still do it. They go to a farm outside London, get one and give it to the godparents. But I never did it. I never gave a chicken to my godparents, nor to my sisters, because my sisters are family. You could give to close family, but if it was a poor family, you didn't do it.

Many people breast fed, but I didn't – they said I was a *vaca seca* – a dry cow! – because I didn't have any milk. If you did breast feed, people told you not to eat some kinds of food, because if you ate badly it would affect the baby. Some people breast-fed until the child was two or three years old, some only up to three months. You can keep on giving it – there's nothing to stop you.

But if you didn't breast feed them, or you didn't have any milk, there was cow's milk, not powder, with water, because the milk by itself is too strong for the baby. You used a bottle, but not a proper baby's bottle – I remember that for my sisters we used drink bottles, such as ones for Coca Cola. They bought the drinks, but they of course didn't give that to the baby! They had a teat they bought from the chemists. Sometimes they fed young animals the same way.

Like I said, if you got pregnant, you had to marry. But maybe you had had an affair. Then sometimes they made abortions for themselves with strong herbs. I remember I went to get herbs one time and the lady said "Are you pregnant?" I said no. She said "Because this one is for pregnant women." They often used black beer – Guinness – they boiled it and drank it with some herbs. If you were in labour, they made a tea with the same herbs, so your baby came quicker. That was the one they also used to help to make an abortion.

They had large families, because they didn't have any choice. If you had sex, you got pregnant. There was no contraception. They lost so many babies, but there was nothing to avoid it. And if you lost the baby, you lost it and nobody knew – you just bled, maybe a month late.

At first there was just one GP for the whole of Santana, and you had to go to their surgery. Then they opened a clinic in a house – an expensive big house, where they had space.

Next they opened a clinic for the mothers, to see the doctors when they were pregnant. But then there was a problem, because the men didn't like it. That was because, when you went to see the doctor, you took your clothes off and you wore a white gown like a nightdress. I still remember how the men were – it was a disaster, they didn't accept it.

But when the baby was born, you went there, straight away, when you came from the hospital. And then they told us about ways to avoid getting pregnant.

A Woman's Place...

With regard to relations between men and women, the society Maria lived in was very different from what it is like in Britain today. The great differences between the two societies have been a recurrent theme in these introductions. But with regard to the time she writes of, we should not be too complacent.

It is true that whereas British women obtained equal voting rights in 1928, Portuguese women had to wait until 1976, with the creation of the new, post-Salazar Constitution. But in the UK the Equal Pay Act only came into force in 1970, with the Sex Discrimination Act being passed after another five years.

Nevertheless, the situation of women in Maria's community was not as strictly determined as, for example, in some more conservative Muslim societies. Women did not have to cover their faces or heads (except in church) and they worked alongside men in the fields. And there were points where young people could meet and talk a little – for instance coming home from church. But any hint of a relationship immediately gave rise to a lot of gossip and sometimes rather malicious talk.

Certainly, as we have seen earlier, to spend time with or court a girl, the boy had to get the permission of her father. And once the girl was married, control very much passed to the man. Maria sees it as "Work – and keep quiet!"

The way it was for women was very different from the life I have now in England. To start with, there was what we wore.

At one time all the women wore a long skirt of wool. Skirts in my time were shorter than the old ladies wore – but they were still under the knee. My grandmother had a long skirt, but my mum never liked a long dress. And they all wore the same style.

My grandmother made skirts from *estufa* – that was the first stage of making *linho* (linen), which was rougher – and she made blouses from *linho,* which was finer and softer. Later, when we had a shop, we bought material – we called it *popelinho (*poplin) – and made a dress, a skirt or knickers. Before that we didn't wear knickers. And I remember that when my grandmother was out and wanted to pee, she just stopped, pulled out her long skirt so it didn't get wet, and did it! She always tried to get us to do the same, but we wouldn't, because we felt it was strange, and we were too embarrassed.

The old ladies used to put a scarf on their head – they bought it in flowery colours. And they wore boots – the shoemaker made them. They were very solid and lasted for a long time. My mum had boots like that, because by tradition women wore boots and a shawl. Later they wore a different sort of shoes, also made by the shoemaker. I had a pair of shoes like that, but my sisters didn't wear them – they wanted more fashionable things.

But the big difference between then and now was in the relations between men and women. In conversations the men talked to the men and the women to women. Even in the church the men went on one side and the women on the other.

And you had to be really careful about being seen with a man. I remember I went to the city by bus one day, and when I came home I sat down behind the driver. Then I saw it was a man who people talked about – they said he went for the girls. I was married by then but I was still so embarrassed – I wondered what people would say.

When we were young, we would talk about boys and say "He's very nice" and when I met Antonio people would say "He is good looking and has nice white teeth." But you just talked in your group; if you talked to a young man, they already thought you were engaged. If you and a young man were working together, they thought he was your boyfriend, and people would say they thought there would be a marriage. When I began working with Antonio, I was also working with a group of girls, and straightaway they spread the news that Antonio was my boyfriend, though there was nothing between us.

I remember a much older man – he was in the Army and he wrote to my parents, because he was my father's friend and god-father of one of his children. The envelope was different from the normal letter. People noticed and said he was writing to me.

Sometimes a young couple would start to go together and then split up. If that happened, the boys did a not very nice thing. When you grow *trigo* (wheat), there is the part we call *saruga* (the beard) or *pragana* (bristles) – that's the same word as we call the whiskers of a cat. Normally we kept it to give to the animals. But if a girl had split up with her boyfriend, other boys went to her street during the night and left what we call a *ramada de saruga* – *ramada* is the word we use when they put flowers on the street during a festival. And to make things worse, it was very hard to sweep up, because it got stuck between the cobblestones.

The men always had the upper hand. Always they had to do everything – we were not allowed to do anything. Well, we had to work, but we were not allowed to make decisions. If they wanted to go somewhere, the wife or even a girlfriend had to follow them. Even if the man decided he didn't want to go to church, you would stay at home. And in the evening the men went to the *taverna* alone, closed the door and stayed inside to talk.

Inside the house it was different. The woman had to look after the children, do the housework, the cooking and keep quiet. And if you didn't look good when you weren't working, they didn't like it, because it looked like they were very poor.

Some women – not that many – were very strong in character. Their man was not very good at thinking and so those women were lucky enough to decide everything. But if the woman was more clever than her husband, they talked about her, and said she wore the trousers. I remember one old lady – people didn't like her, because her husband had to do everything she said.

And people called such men bad names and said he was not a proper man. Sometimes people who had travelled had learned different ways, such as doing things around the house. But they soon stopped, because of what people said about them. I remember one man and his wife had travelled. At first, the man would go to buy things, or fetch water from the tank. Then people called him *maricas* (queer, poof, not a man).

When we were in England, my husband started to help in the house, but any time we went back to Madeira, he stopped and never did anything. I can see now that the women did not have the power to go forward.

Health

Possibly the most startling difference between the wider world and Maria's community was in medicine. In the 1960s all the major transplant operations were performed for the first time. In the decade after 1965 doctors came to have the diagnostic advantages of ultrasound, MRI, CAT and PET scans. And the life of many women was transformed by the arrival fo the contraceptive pill in 1960.

Maria's account of medicine shows how different life was in Santana at that time. To begin with, there was no health service and the only free care was from the nuns. And hospital care was a long journey away. You only went there – or to the doctor – if you really had to. So most of the care was what we would now call "folk medicine." For instance, many modern Polish women still recommend the use of cabbage leaves in the way described by Maria, for high temperatures and period pains.

It would be very easy to find this quaint, or be sceptical about some of the things she describes. Some things seem magical, or to put trust in numbers, such as seven. People certainly found support in their faith, and modern research has proved how powerful one's mental state is in healing. It certainly makes sense to build up the strength of a new mother, and breast feeding women are still advised to avoid foods that can upset a newborn baby's stomach.

Also, many of us have experienced the effectiveness of good massage or similar techniques, and it would be hard not to agree with her that some people seem to have "green fingers" in such matters.

But before dismissing some of the more unusual things she describes, such as the ceremony of the willow tree, it is worth noting that the University of Maryland Medical Centre cites research (for details see: https://umm.edu/health/medical/altmed/herb/willow-bark) *on both the proven and claimed benefits of willow bark. This contains salicin, a chemical similar to aspirin. So it is an effective treatment of inflammation and pain. Researchers have found that the plant has other valuable chemicals, such as polyphenols and flavonoids, which have further medical uses (for instance, antioxidants). Interestingly though, the article notes that "children under the age of 18 should not take willow bark", because it can have adverse effects on the young.*

A similar situation applies to the oak bark bath described by Maria. This contains tannins which have astringent and antiseptic properties, and are recommended by herbal medicine practitioners for various complaints, including eczema.

Nor is it necessary to share a belief in miracles, in order to accept that olive leaves can also have beneficial effects. They contain oleuropin, which has been found to lower blood pressure, at least in animal experiments, as well as elenolic acid which some researchers believe is effective in combatting bacteria, viruses, and fungi.

Maria also tells of using the "juice" (latex) of the fig tree to cure warts. Science has shown this to be effective, including with warts on the teats of cows (US Journal of Veterinary Medicine, 2003).

Less desirable was the mercurio *medicine. In earlier centuries it was believed that it could cure venereal diseases, and it is still used in various parts of the world in the form of mercury sublimate (chemical formula $HgCl_2$) as an antiseptic for wounds. It is now prohibited in many countries, due to the recognition of serious effects caused by exposure to the chemical.*

It was very different in those days if you were sick – not at all like now in England, where you have the NHS. If you went to the nuns, you didn't have to pay, but with the doctor you did – the doctors were rich – so you only went to the doctor when the patient was very ill.

And here you have hospitals. Then they had to walk for hours to go to the hospital in the city, so if they went, they were very ill. The Germans built it in the First World War. Now we have another we call the "New Hospital." When they had cars, the sick person had to go from where they lived to Santana, and then in the car to the city.

Because it cost a lot for medicines, they often used herbs. Some of the old people knew a lot about that. For instance, from trees in the mountains they got bay leaves. But they needed to know which were better – they have to be more mature. They kept the herbs that were good in the house in a vase or a pot and made a lot of teas with them.

They used the leaves of trees too. At one time my son Victor had very bad eczema. The patches of skin itched a lot, so he scratched them until they bled and he couldn't sleep. Nothing seemed to work, so I got the leaves of an oak tree, and boiled them with some other herbs and gave him baths in the juice. That seemed to work.

Some people also went to the woods to collect leaves from a special olive tree. This was because it grew in a place where people went to pray. They said that many years before a girl had seen the Virgin Mary, so the local people made a shrine with a statue of the Virgin in it. Then there was a very bad storm and this caused an avalanche. It destroyed all the woods around, but the statue itself was not touched. People thought this was a miracle, and so they believed that the leaves of that tree could make miracles.

We didn't have special diets, like they do now. At that time you ate anything that was around – there was not much choice.

When someone had a temperature, for example if a child was too hot, they put a wet cloth on the forehead – they even used milk to wet it. And they also used some leaves, such as cabbage. You got big cabbage leaves and then put them on your stomach. The leaves got dry, because you were too hot. It was almost like it cooked the cabbage, and that took the heat away.

If you had a pain, if you were a child, you had a massage – some people were good at it. Sometimes the stomach got hard, and instead of taking medicine, because they didn't have much at that time they gave a massage. They did that to every child and the child felt better. They went to the person three times, or five or nine, but not an even number.

I believe it helped. I remember I took my brother and my sisters to a lady – we had one lady in Santana who did massages. You had to walk a long way to get to her, but she was quite understanding. I was the oldest, so I had to carry my sisters there. That lady had something like green fingers. They had a way of touching until they found something hard, and then they pressed. They used olive oil – it makes your hands move easily.

If you had a headache, the families made a tea with herbs and lemons – if you didn't have a lemon, you used the lemon tree leaves or orange leaves.

For diarrhoea, they made a drink with flour to make it thicker. It was not nice to drink but it settled down your stomach to stop the problem. It did not work all the time, but often it helped.

When you were constipated, there were a lot of things you could do. You could have a massage. But sometimes you drank hot wine or *aguardente* with lemon. Another thing we did was to boil the "whiskers" of sweet corn, and to sit over a bowl of the liquid, to allow the steam to work on you.

If you had an ear problem, you got apples and put the juice in your ears. Or you used olive oil. They warmed it. But it is dangerous, so it was just warmed a bit and you dropped it in the ear and the dirty stuff came out.

With the eyes, say they were red or painful, you had a plant you could use – we called it *balso*. If you had an eye problem, they dropped the juice into the eyes – they still do it.

Sometimes you got a problem of white skin between your toes – it could be very painful. They put ashes there – we called them *frieiras* – to dry it up.

For a tooth pain the thing I remember most was *aguardente*. You gargled it in your mouth and then swallowed it. But for the pain there was not much else they could do at that time. And if you use the *arguardente* too often, it damages your teeth and the gums and roots, because it is very strong.

There were treatments for warts. I had one on my hand. You find a fig tree and when you break it, it gives some kind of milk – not much, but you squeezed it out and you used it a few times. Another thing was when you baked bread and the oven was hot, you threw salt over your shoulder into the oven. It made a lot of crackling noise. Then people said the warts went away.

When you had a small cut, it would heal on its own. I don't know when the pharmacy opened, but it was there when I was young, and there was some medicine like blood. It was called *mercurio* and when you had a cut, you used that. And I remember we also had a powder and you dropped that on top of the cut and it healed.

If you twisted your arm or leg or it got swollen, they got the leaves of some herbs. They put them on it and it went away. Another thing was they put wine vinegar on the swelling or bruise. Sometimes they put salt as well, and sometimes just the vinegar.

When a person was very sick or injured and they had to take him to the town, they had a special thing they used. I remember my grandparents had a wooden pole and linen cloth, but it had to be strong like the cloth you used for making mats. They tied it up at each end and made a sort of hammock (we called it *rede*), like some people have in their garden now, and hung it from the pole. One man held each end of the pole and the two men carried the patient. They had walking sticks, because they needed them to go over the hills.

Women often had a period pain, because at that time they worked on the land and got wet, and they got cold, and they worked without shoes. I remember that you toasted a slice of bread in the hot embers – not a fire with a flame. They boiled wine and soaked the bread in the wine and put it on your belly and they brought a towel and they covered it. The wine gets warmer for a while and so you feel warm inside and that takes the cold away and the pain goes. I did that. It had to be at night time, because you had to go to bed and cover yourself well, and sometimes you got a bit sweaty. But you had to keep yourself as hot as you could.

We had a lot of medicines. One was the seeds of the *linho* plant – we called it *linhaça* – it's smaller than wheat. We boiled it and it came all together like a sort of porridge. To make the pain go away, you put it in a cloth and put it on your belly, because it keeps warm for a while. And you had old clothes to cover your stomach too. It was not nice, because it was slimy, you know, like the trails snails make. Even now you can buy *linhaça* for some medicines.

If the periods didn't come normally, they made tea with a special herb for the woman to drink. But it was not advised for the women who might be pregnant, because it can bring on a miscarriage.

I remember that when I was young, the people who were ill for a long time stayed at home, and the family had to look after them, while they were waiting to die. When the person was close to dying, the patient would be put in a room just for them. Then people stayed with the dying person during the night. If it was not one of the family, the neighbours often came to help. At the end, before the person died, people would come to be company for the family, or to let them sleep a while. And they lit a candle. At the moment when the person looked about to die, they need-ed to put a candle next to them. But sometimes it took a long time before the person did die, so to make the candle last longer, they took olive oil, and put in a piece of material for a wick, and then put the candle in that and lit it. That way it lasts longer.

We called the candle *candeia*. It had been blessed – it was from the church. Before Easter Saturday, at night, there was a mass, when they blessed them. The ones who went to the mass held a candle and took it home, because it had been blessed. They kept it for special occasions, and especially for when someone died. But it was not only for that. For instance, if there was bad weath-er, like a storm, they lit the candle.

There were some very special customs to do with health. One was if the baby had a problem with its belly button. Of course, when the baby is born, they cut it, and sometimes it did not heal well. Then they took the child on 24 June and found a *vimieiro* (willow) tree. They cut the trees for wicker in March, but they left one or two branches for 24 June. They cut the tree in the middle and they opened it. But the top and the bottom had still to be joined together, so it made a hole in the tree, not a split. Then two children pass the baby through the tree. They have to be called Maria and João, because 24 June is the *Dia de São João* (St John's Day). And they have to be virgins, so of course they have to be children! They say a prayer. I did it once for a child of our neighbour. I don't remember the prayer, but I do remember the way they said *"Tomala, Maria"* (Hold her, Maria) and they said a prayer *"In nome de São João* (in the name of St John) cure this baby." And I had to hold the baby and pass her to the boy, and I said "Pass the baby to João in the name of São João" and so on. But the baby should not touch the *vimieiro* tree. We passed it a few times and after that they closed the tree. If it seals properly, then the baby will heal, but if doesn't seal, because the wound needs more time, they need to do it again the next year.

Another thing I did was when my first son, David, was a baby. We think he had asthma, so we went to Madeira to the doctors, and they sent him to Funchal, but he wasn't cured. But people gave me a lot of different ideas and I tried them.

One was the *eucalipto* tree, which grows quickly. I went with David to the woods and put him against the tree, and against his height I put a nail. They said the tree would grow and as it did, slowly he would be cured, because the tree grows, and it will take the illness from him. But it had to be in a place where he wouldn't pass for seven years.

Another thing I did for him was that I took some of his dirty clothes, and dug the ground and put them in the ground and covered them. They said when the clothes got rotten, he would be cured. So it had to be a natural fibre, not nylon, because nylon doesn't rot. And again it had to be some area he wouldn't pass for seven years. That was fine, because when the child is small, you know that he won't go to that area during that time.

I did that for him and another thing was with my door. You make a small hole in the door, at the size he is, cut off a bit of his hair, and put the hair in the hole. Then you cover it. He can pass there any time, but again when he grows, the illness will be cured.

What they advised me, I tried. I don't know if it is good medicine, but thank God he was cured. Perhaps it helped.

There was one thing they did when the child didn't walk properly and took a long time to start walking, because it had weak legs. When they made wine, they put the child into the wine – they did that to my sister, Linda. I don't know if they kept the child in there for a while or not. But they washed them in the wine, because it was new. The strange thing is that the wine is cold, but it doesn't feel cold like water.

A Mind Diseas'd

Canst thou not minister to a mind diseas'd?
Macbeth, Act V, scene i

All societies have people whose mental state is different from that of the majority. In modern Britain there is a lot of knowledge about how people's minds are affected, and how to help them. And there is much more sympathy than there used to be for those who suffer from mental problems.

But Maria describes a very different world, in which these things were not understood and could seem to come from nowhere, for no apparent reason. So often there was fear, and things could get to a point where people had to be restrained. And as has happened throughout history, when the sufferer's behaviour is very antisocial, this is sometimes explained by the activity of troubled souls, or possession by evil spirits.

When people had mental problems, it was very different from now. People always used strong words – they called them "crazies" or *louco* (mad).

We also had people who now you would say have learning difficulties. At that time they called them *bruto* or *brutinho* or *louquinho*. It meant they were not clever, and people called them names. Sometimes they didn't call them by their Christian name – instead they made nicknames for them. For instance, I have a relation by marriage who can neither hear or speak. So people always call him *o mudo* (the dumb boy). But in fact he wasn't born like that – he got meningitis, which damaged his brain.

In those days the family used to leave them at home, when they went somewhere – the person stayed behind – or in some cases they just went out with the family to the church. They never were involved with normal people. They did work, though, on the land or at home. Sometimes they could be very useful, but often they were just slow. But people didn't push them. They worked, and they could work harder, because they focused on the task.

Sometimes they got married, but then it was with another person like them. I remember there was a man – he was not a perfect man, but he was good looking. He worked on the land and he could make jokes. He was very popular because he worked everywhere. They didn't care about his mental ability – they invited him to work because he worked hard. He wanted to marry a woman who was less clever than him. The priest didn't want to marry them, but the man fought for it and I think he insisted, so the priest married them.

If a person was depressed, I don't think other people did much to help at that time. They blamed the person and said "You are lazy" or "You're crazy." The same was true if they were stressed. I don't think people understood about these things then. If you were ill, they understood, but they didn't see anything when it was a mental problem.

There were people who said "I'm going to kill myself", but usually they didn't. But always when a person did kill themself, it was because they couldn't hold their problems. It was easy to kill yourself, if you really wanted to do it – often they hanged themselves. But I remember one guy who went to a place far away with a huge waterfall.

Or they might drink chemicals. That happened with a man who was a builder. One of his men fell and was killed. That man had split up with his wife, because she didn't look after him properly. But at that time by the law, the employer had to pay compensation. Then the wife wanted more and more, and so he couldn't cope and got drunk all the time. In the end he drank poison, because he had so many troubles.

A person who committed suicide could be buried in the cemetery, but not with the full religious ceremony. When someone committed suicide, people said about that person *"Não se salva"* (He won't be saved). At the funeral in the church, some priests were very strictly religious and just said the words "Pray for him" and so on, because it is a mortal sin. But some priests might be more sympathetic and say they "had a feeling" that the person would be all right.

I remember some women had babies, and afterwards they got into a bad state, and people said *"Esta louca"* (She's mad). Nowadays they don't say that. It can happen very quickly They became aggressive, they shouted, they called everyone names, they told lies and sometimes they would fight. But it wasn't easy to get treatment. They were sent a mental institution in the city, but it wasn't a nice place, and they didn't like to be there. In those days we called it *a casa dos loucos* (the mad house) or *o trapicho* – that was a rougher sort of word. Now people prefer to say *a casa de saude* (the house of health).

In the early stages of mental illness, we didn't have support then. But when a person got advanced mental illness, if the family found out the person was mental, they went to the doctor and told him what was happening. And the doctor would find a way to send them to the city to the mental hospital. But other times they got in trouble, and threw things and so on, so people called the police, and they arrested them and took them to the mental hospital.

But always when the person was ill, they never accepted it, and they never wanted to go for treatment. So to take them to the hospital, the family needed to lie to them. Then when the patient found out what had been done, they said "You took me there" and got aggressive and destroyed things. They stole things and broke things. They even cut the ropes that tied the cows in the stable, so the cows wandered away. It was a sort of revenge.

I knew one family where there was a lady – she hated all the family because she them blamed for sending her to the treatment. She would shout and she would say things that were not true, but people would hear it and they believed it.

Some people saw things or heard strange noises. If they thought the house was haunted, they brought holy water and sprinkled it in the house. They took the palm leaf cross from Palm Sunday, and some herbs, and cut them up and put them in a tray or dish. They added rosemary, and the skin of garlic, and made the mixture into the shape of a cross. Then they set fire to it, so there was a little fire that made a lot of smoke, like incense in the church. They carried the fire around the house, so the smoke went everywhere. The priest came and gave a blessing, and the people prayed for the bad spirit to go away. If it didn't go, they called the priest to bless the house again.

I remember once a lady – they brought some flowers from the cemetery to her house. But they say that you can't take what is in the cemetery. Then people said there was a lot of noise, and that was because they had brought a bad spirit back from the cemetery. So they had to take flowers back, or throw them away.

Sometimes it could be a place that felt bad. When I was in Jersey, there were people from Madeira there. They took me to show me this place where there was a statue – it is very big, made in bronze, but it doesn't look like a proper person. And there is a pond, but the grass around is not clean. The people called it the *buraco do diabo* (the Devil's pit). A *buraco* is a dark, gloomy place, for instance a dark lane, or even some houses. I wasn't scared, but I thought it was not a nice place to be.

Some people saw things. They could be visions that were good, angels or the Virgin Mary. But sometimes it was a bad experience – they saw bad things – maybe a figure with a big body like an animal, or something black, or a scary face, or a *bruxa* (witch).

Some people believed there were very bad spirits and that some people had a spirit like that in them. Often people said "Her mother had it and she got it from her mother." Then everyone avoided them – they didn't trust them, and they didn't like them. If something happened, they believed it was because the person made it happen to you. Maybe their hair had been cut, and they believed that the bad spirit had done it. Or if your son became ill, you thought that a spirit made it happen. Another thing was that a person could find strange bruises on their legs or arms that looked like they were tooth-marks. I remember this happened to my mother. Then people said that the *bruxa* had bitten you, and that you must rub it with garlic, because the *bruxa* doesn't like garlic!

When a person was believed to have a bad spirit in them, people said it took longer for them to die. Then they didn't want to be around the dying person. That was because they believed that the person couldn't die before they had passed the spirit to someone else. The spirit was called a *mando* (power). So the dying person would say *"Pega, pega "* (take it, take it). They seemed like they wanted to give you something, but you couldn't see anything in their hand. But people said that if someone held the person's hand, the spirit would pass from them, and they could die afterwards in peace. I don't know if this is really true – I've never seen it – but it's what people say.

Politics

As we have seen before, Maria's village does not seem to have suffered too much from the Salazar regime – she puts it down to it being a remote, small agricultural community. Also, the demands of living meant that there was not much time for politics.

An important part of the State's control was the PIDE, or Polícia Internacional e de Defesa do Estado *(International Police and State Defence). It was a security service established in 1933. Experts feel that PIDE was one of the most effective such organisations ever. This seems to have been due to a network of secret cells and agents. They also encouraged ordinary people to inform on others, typically through money and other rewards.*

In the 1974 Revolution the only people killed were shot by agents who had been cornered in the PIDE headquarters in Lisbon. This was the last place taken by the revolutionary groups, which gave time for most of the records to be destroyed. Most of the agents escaped and either fled to Spain (then still under Franco) or other places, including, as Maria shows, Britain.

They called it PIDE under Salazar. Before I got married, I wasn't really aware of it. We had a police station in Santana, but because there were not many people and they lived on farms, it was not very political.

But Antonio was more aware of politics than me, and when we got married, he talked about these things. I remember after I was married, Antonio showed me a man who was on the bus – he was secret police. He didn't show it, but people found out somehow and they were careful about talking when he was around. Antonio said there were often plain clothes police on the bus. I wasn't aware because I was never involved.

I learned more because we had a neighbour who talked a lot with my father in the 80s about the past and about the secret police. For example, when there was war in other countries, they took the men to do the fighting. The men didn't want to go and so they hid – in the stables and so on. But always someone passed the news to the police, and you didn't know who had done that.

For the same reason many Portuguese people went from Madeira to other countries – to Lisbon or to France. But the secret police got to know these things, and then someone was waiting for the people who went away, when they arrived. But it was always difficult to find out who had told them.

I remember another time there was a young man – he was younger than me, and he was in the Army in Funchal. He escaped and went back home. When the police came, he could see them coming – but they still caught him.

After the Revolution a lot of people were very happy. They caught the people that had done those things. But then a lot of them disappeared. They ran away to other countries, because they knew they were guilty. I remember, there was a lady working in St Pancras Hospital, the place where I also worked. and she had been involved with the regime. So she never went back to the country for many years, because she knew she would be caught.

In those times the police didn't always do their duty. They could do things that were not right, but nobody complained then. If you were a friend of theirs , you could get away with things, and you never had a problem. It was like at the bank – if you knew someone, you got served first – it still happens. We said: *Que tem padrinhos, não morre sem alma.* (Whoever has a godfather, doesn't die without a soul). Now it is more strict for the police. They go around, deal with parking, stop cars and so on.

Then and Now...

This is a time when many people look back nostalgically to a simpler, more honest world that they feel they lived in when they were young. So at the end of the interviews I asked Maria how she viewed those times and now: was life better then, or worse? I had assumed that, because she often speaks of the happy times she remembers, she would feel that much has been lost.

This was partly true, but in fact her opinions are much more complex than a simple dream of a beautiful rural life. She says that many things were accepted because people knew nothing else. "We didn't have the opportunity to think a different way."

But she also feels strongly that there are many gains in modern life, for old people, and certainly for her, as a woman. Above all, for her, life is better now, "because you have chances and you can change things."

In those days we did work hard and we were poor and did not have a lot of food. So we didn't waste anything. If you were a child, you didn't play with toys – you played with natural things, and you sang, and danced around in a circle.

Then there were the special days – we really enjoyed making a procession, you know, like the one in my village – the procession of Mary. Even if it rained, we went. The procession started from the church, which was a long way off, but we wanted to go and people said "It's time to go – don't be late!" And you would pray and you would sing. It was a good life at that time.

Also, when you were working on the land, you sang – you didn't need to know how to sing! – and you shouted to your friends – the people on the other side of the valley. It was natural, and more lively than most work now!

And there was not so much worry. So if you had a small cut, you put on a bandage and you carried on working.

It was a life where you talked to your neighbours, perhaps because you didn't see an alternative. You didn't share your life with the people in Santana, just those in our area, Silveira. You saw the Santana people, but you didn't get very close to them, because it was like walking now to Kings' Cross to go to church, or further. You met them there, but when the church finished, you came home.

We got a lot of pleasure from special presents, because they were rare. For instance, for us at that time it was normal that you didn't have a watch. So I really remember my first watch. I had it when I was fourteen years old. It was my present for my Confirmation – my godmother gave me a dress – a top and skirt – and a watch – a big, big present! It had a strap in brown and *numbers* – it wasn't points or even Roman numbers. But they had to teach me how to tell the time. I remember they said "With this hand, this way you go up and this way you go down. So this is twenty to and this is ten past." It was a big surprise – my godparents were very good, not just to me, but to my brother as well.

These days the children stay inside a lot or they go in a car with their parents. But then the children were very free – the door was open. Of course they had to keep the small children inside – there were channels carrying water to the fields, so it would have been dangerous for them to be out alone. I remember in my father's kitchen, he cut the door in half, so you could close the bottom with a bolt. That kept the small children inside the kitchen. But after my son was born, when he could walk, I left the door shut but not locked, so he used to get out and cross the street to my mum's house.

When the children were still quite small, they took them to the land. They sat on the ground and if they couldn't walk, they stayed there and the parents carried on working. The very small children stayed at home, and slept long hours in a baby cot, to make sure they didn't fall. The parents went to work – it wasn't like now, controlled every second. But it wasn't bad because if the children cried, there were the neighbours and they knew where the parents were and would say things like "Oh *maezinha*, she's gone to bring water" or "She's gone to give food to the workers." Everyone knew what you were doing, where you had gone. Now it's more private, but still the people watch and think "They went that way, so they've gone into Santana" and so on.

Another thing I ask myself is "Why did the children have to go away and not be with the adults who were talking?" That was very wrong. It's better now.

How we dress and how much you show has changed a lot. When I was in Jersey, before I came here, it was completely new for me. In Jersey I never went to the beach. But in summer when I finished work on a farm, I went to visit my aunties at a hotel where they worked. The people in Jersey had big houses with gardens, because they were rich people. And they lay around in swimming costumes. I was on my own, and I was so embarrassed and shocked, because I never saw anything like that, so I never expected to see naked people – well, they weren't naked of course. Now it is different, but at that time I was nervous and walked by. I felt it was wrong, because I didn't have communication with other different people.

In some ways it is really much better now, because to keep these things secret is not good. I think to hide yourself up to the neck and under the knees is not necessary.

However, it should be different when you go to the church. If you are a woman, you shouldn't have short sleeves. But people now don't respect that, especially the younger generation. I don't think you need to cover everything, but you need to show some respect. So there are bad things and good things.

That's one thing these days – people have lost a lot of respect. Before, you didn't need to be told – you had the respect, but now it's not like that. When you spoke to a teacher or someone superior, you said *senhor*. For instance, a lady who was old or middle aged, you called her *senhora*, but not always. Sometimes you used a special form of their name, like for *Maria* – *Marizinha*, or for *Ana* – *Aninhas*. It was a sign of respect, but also of affection. You didn't call her *Ana* or *Senhora Aninhas* – if you said *Senhora Maria* or *Senhora Ana*, it was more formal. But if you said something not appropriate, they told your parents, who gave you a strong slap in your face.

Even with your family, my aunties, my grandparents, my cousins or even a neighbour and with adults, you needed to speak to them in the right way. And that was true with your parents-in-law. You were supposed to call them the same as your own parents (*mãe, pãe*). But I didn't like them, so I always avoided doing it – it seemed wrong to me – after all, they weren't really my parents.

In the family, the first time in the day when you saw them, you gave a special greeting – for my mother it was *mãe a bencão* (Bless you, mother). You didn't say it every time you saw them, just the first time, even if it was the evening. Nowadays many people give a kiss, but in my family we still say it.

In Silveira it's better with electricity, because it is much brighter. But at that time we didn't see the difference. My aunt, she lived in Funchal, and when she came to our house with her children, they said they couldn't see. We didn't understand – we could see and we did things in the darkness. You could touch and feel your way. There was just a small light on the table.

We could walk for hours, even in darkness – if it was very black we said *"preto como o carvão"* (as black as coal). It says in the dictionary that you can say *"escuro como o breu"* (as dark as pitch), but I have never heard that. When you wanted to do things at night, you would choose a night with moonlight. With the moon you can dig a hole or cut wood or saw. You could even wash your clothes in the tank. When I was young, I did the washing in the night sometimes, maybe because the next day I had to do something. You just had to imagine when you had done enough, because you couldn't see properly. So when the clothes were very dirty, you scrubbed them a lot!

But when the electricity came – woooo ! – we were so excited!

Now they don't work on the farms, or if they do, they don't work at night. In my parents' house we didn't do much work at night, but some people did a lot. Sometimes it was that they didn't want others to know that they did things in a secret way. I remember one man, he always had good, big sweet potatoes. He dug during the day and took the grass out – but he put fertiliser on them during the night or early in the morning, so that the people didn't know how they grew so well.

Nowadays a good thing is that they have special places for the old people – like a day room – and they have activities for them. In the old days your aunties or your grandparents would stay with the family. If it was difficult for them to walk, they stayed indoors all the time – there was nowhere to go and so they had no exercise. They just cooked a lot of potatoes for the family.

Now they do lot of things for the old people that are very good. There are activities – singing, dancing, playing cards, and maybe painting or making things they never did in their lives – for example, many of them have never made a dress. At the beginning not many people went there. It was difficult for them – it seemed strange. But some people were in a state of mind to go and they encouraged the others. It's a good thing for them, because otherwise when you get old, you can't do anything – you just stay at home. They feel more energetic after they start this.

Another thing is that here you get different cultures, and come to understand how you need to respect each other. You work with people and you learn bit by bit. You learn that they are wearing something strange or different, not because they are crazy or don't have brains, maybe they have to dress like that. But the people here sometimes take a lot of advantage in those cases. It is also much better now back home – not in the country – but in the city it is more or less like here.

It is much better being a woman here, now, in England. A good thing now is that people are together, women and men. Before you were always separate. Even if you worked together on the land, you had to be careful at that time – the men couldn't be with the women. If you had a conversation with men they said "Oh, she's too much." Now it is not like that and that is very good, because you meet each other. Even when we got married, why didn't we speak together? Now it is much better, because it's not just that the men go on one side and the women on another. We can trust each other and we can enjoy the conversation.

And there were no chances to change. For instance, if you wanted to work in the city, if you couldn't get a job, you could go to work in a house, like an au pair. But it only happened if the girl didn't have a father, or her parents had died, or her mother had got together with another man. Some people didn't like those children, because if girls went to the city, they would get a bad reputation. That work was only for very poor or dishonest people. People said "When you cross the boundary to Faial (a neighbouring area), you lose your respect." Really, you had to get married, before you could leave your parents' house.

I know that we were very poor and we didn't have heating and electricity and technology. On the other hand you saw it that way – you were used to it – it was all you knew. You knew you had to work to get things, and if you didn't, you didn't get them. It was when they opened the roads that everything changed. Until then the people in Santana – at least in some parts – had a different life. They thought we were very rough and dirty people. But the real reason was that we had to walk along dirty and muddy paths to get to church, so it was impossible to keep your clothes and shoes clean.

There are good things now, different things, and now no one in Madeira wants that life any more, except in festivals. But at that time we didn't have the opportunity to think in a different way.

I think that the worst thing was that at that time there was no way to change your life. So life is better now, because you have chances and you can change things. What can I say ? They had no other way – no chance to change their life.

Postscript

In 1979 Maria left the island for the first time to join her husband, who was working in Jersey. That was when her life began to change. But that's another story...

Background 1 – Some Portuguese History

The Roman writers Pliny and Plutarch refer to Atlantic islands which are believed to be Madeira and nearby Porto Santo. They were known as "the Isles of the Blest." The islands were uninhabited.

The modern history of Madeira dates from 1419 when the Portuguese sea captains, João Gonçalves Zarco and Tristão Vaz Teixeira, were caught in a storm. They found an island where they were able to take shelter, which they called Porto Santo (Holy Harbour) as thanks for their escape from shipwreck. The name Ilha da Madeira (Madeira Island or "island of wood") is known to have been in use by 1433.

The King of Portugal took possession of the islands in 1420, and from that point they began to be settled. The settlers first produced grain for export to the mainland, and a little later, sugar cane. Since the 17th Century Madeira has also been known for its unique type of wine.

The voyages which led to the discovery are a major part of Portuguese history. In their caravels – a ship well suited to coastal navigation and to sailing inland – the captains edged down the West coast of Africa, rounded the Cape of Good Hope, and explored the Indian Ocean. Vasco da Gama arrived in India in 1498, and in 1530 Goa was declared to be the capital of Portuguese India. That made possible a dramatic shift in the spice trade. The Portuguese continued to sail eastwards and finally reached Japan in 1543.

The result of the explorations was the creation of the Portuguese Empire, of which the most notable areas were Angola, Mozambique, Goa and Macau. Decolonisation only came in the 20th century.

Portuguese rule ended in Goa in 1961 after a brief armed conflict with the Indian Armed Forces.

The republic of Mozambique was until 1975 a Portuguese colony. This was because in 1498 the explorer Vasco da Gama had first reached the Mozambican coast. Then in 1544 Lourenço Marques explored the area that is now Maputo Bay. He settled there and a town (mentioned by Maria) was given his name; this was changed to Maputo after independence.

The latter came partly as a result of the Carnation Revolution of 1975 in Continental Portugal and partly because from 1964 the Front for the Liberation of Mozambique (FRELIMO) had conducted a guerrilla war.

At least in theory Mozambique, according to official policy, was not a colony but instead a part of the "pluricontinental and multiracial nation" of Portugal. In 1951 various colonies were combined into a single overseas province, Moçambique, which thus became an integral part of Portugal. Despite the fascist orientation of the Salazar government, his policy was to Europeanise and assimilate the African population, who in principle would ultimately become full citizens with full political rights. Indeed Salazar himself liked to say that that any Portuguese African could in theory become a member of the Portuguese government, and even the President. Certainly, there are a large number of people of African descent now living in Portugal and also a fair number who have migrated to Britain, since Portugal became part of the EU.

Maria went to school during the Salazar regime (the Estado Novo*), or more precisely, during that and the regime which continued after his death in 1970 until the Carnation Revolution of 25 April 1974.*

Dr Salazar did build a primary school in every town, but there were only four years of compulsory education. This was because he believed that further education was not suitable for most people – he claimed that it destroyed their traditional and religious values. He felt that higher education should be reserved for a minority (of which he, originally a professor at the University of Coimbra, naturally was one). These attitudes were reflected in slogans of the time such as "Blessed are those who forget their first letters and return to the shovel !" and "To teach how to read is to corrupt the essence of our race !"

Background 2 – How Flour Is Produced

When it is ripe, the wheat is harvested. First the stalks are cut up to be dried and so become straw. It is distinct from hay, which is grass which has been cut, dried and stored to be used as animal fodder.

The main purpose of growing wheat is to obtain flour, so the heads of the plant first undergo threshing, which loosens the grain (the seeds) from the surrounding material (the husks). The latter is known as the chaff. This is followed by winnowing, which separates the wheat (grain) from the chaff. The familiar saying comes from the Bible (Matthew 3;12) : "...he will clear his threshing floor and gather his wheat into the barn, but the chaff he will burn with unquenchable fire."

Maria describes the production of flour, which is done by milling (grinding) the grains. Heavy rollers grind up the seeds, which then separate into three components: wheat bran, wheat germ and white flour. These are then separated by sieving.

Bran is the hard outer layers of the grain. Note that chaff is coarse, scaly material surrounding the grain, whereas bran is part of the grain itself.

The germ is the original reproductive part of the seed. It is used as a part of whole grain flours. The inner part (kernel) of the grain, technically the endosperm, is the source of white wheat flour.

Acknowledgements

We wish to express our gratitude and thanks to:

Jeff Haynes,Reg Parks and Frances Lee for invaluable advice and help on book production for the first edition.

Myra Roet for cover photograph of a Madeira coastline.

ELM VILLAGE ARTS
publications

To make contact with the publishers or their authors
in the first instance please
email:

EVApublications@outlook.com

Follies, Fools, and Garlands is about a world of secrets and manipulation. It is also a complicated love story. The central actions of the novel take place during the Cold War of the 1960s, and in a society where upper-class values of the gentry begin to lose their place to the upwardly mobile *nouveau riche*. Anthony Ashley-Chetwyne, narrator and 'son of the privileged', joins the legal profession. Whilst a young barrister he becomes engaged as a junior to an experienced QC in a case of espionage; a member of the House of Commons has been selling secrets to Czechoslovak agents in London. That involvement connects him to behind-the-scene security and intelligence issues and a variety of characters involved in those classified worlds. These include 'Miss K', as she is first known, whose work with the security service crosses Anthony's path both professionally and personally. In that service she connects also with William, a friend of Anthony's from Oxford days. Both she and William are posted to Prague, William with a mission to 'turn' a senior member of the Czech state security, hers of a very different nature. There are surprising twists of narrative and a cast of authentic characters to capture the reader's imagination. Told with wit and humour, the novel as a whole explores themes of deception, lies, secrets, and the concealments of its characters within both their personal and public lives. Whilst probing the edges of the spy thriller, this is a novel concerned above all with the complexities and duplicities of relationships within the febrile nature of trust.

"Follies, Fools, and Garlands **is a wonderful story, an exquisite satire, beautifully told."** — *Ron Smith*, author and former publisher.

"Unputdownable." — *James Gordon*, novelist.

Some reader reviews of Follies, Fools, and Garlands

A remarkable book situated in the 1960s in the Cold War in Europe. Though located in a murky setting – full of secrets, lies and manipulation – in its subtle comments on class and the relationship between the sexes, it goes well beyond the spy genre. *Follies, Fools, and Garlands* cleverly intertwines the secrets, lies and manipulation of the outside world with the personal world(s) of the major characters. This is achieved through wry and astute humour, none so more than in the analysis of the relationship between men and women. The reflections, for example, on the difference between falling in love and falling in lust are very funny indeed. Gardiner also makes some fascinating comments about the use of alcohol in various other settings, again with great humour. The story itself is intriguing – and I won't be the only reader to guess wrongly on both eventual events as well as the major players – yet it is the analysis of the several flawed and duplicitous characters that stand out. The writing just effortlessly flows.Heavily recommended but a warning. Do not read unless you are certain you have no other demands on your time. A truly compelling read, a novel that goes well beyond the simple cold war genre and will make you ponder, think…and laugh.   — *L. Garner*

A masterpiece. A carefully crafted book in which the author leads us into and beyond the prime story, which is itself insightfully told. A book that eloquently highlights the difference between love and lust... and perhaps how little care can be behind both. Reading it will make you laugh and question.   — *Isabella Anders*

This is an unusual book... it gave a real flavour of the chaotic life style of those who work for the intelligence services and not knowing who you can really trust.   — *Geoff Hopkins*

Great read. This novel is an interesting take on the 'spooks' of the Cold War. It dwells on the personal relationships between agents rather than on their spying activities. Mysterious people appear, disappear and reappear throughout the narrative. They rarely tell each other the truth, and the rather 'Oxbridge' language helps sustain the mystery. One is reminded of the spy scandals of the Cold War period – Burgess and Maclean, Profumo *et al*. This is an intelligent read that keeps you guessing to the end, and even then you may not be too clear on who's who. Most enjoyable.   — *P Barrett*

A really good read with a storyline and characters that grabbed your interest and attention so that you were really keen to know what happens next. I really did enjoy this book... a great achievement... I would certainly recommend it to anyone who likes a gripping tale.   — *Margaret H*

Follies, Fools, and Garlands is available to order from Amazon and all bookshops @ £10.99

Kindle version available from Amazon @ £4.99

ISBN: 978-1-9160457-2-9

17536034R10087